A WATCHMAN'S WARNING

Christianity
Mis-sold

by

Leon Gosiewski

Cover design copyright © 2015 by Maurice Wylie Media

Published by Maurice Wylie Media, Bethel Media House, Tobermore, Magherafelt, Northern Ireland BT45 5SG (UK)

Publishers' statement: Throughout this book the love for our God is such that whenever we refer to Him we acknowledge with Capitals. On the other hand when referring to the devil we refuse to acknowledge him with any honour to the point of violating the grammatical rule of a withheld capital.

www.mauricewyliemedia.com

Create | Brand | Establish

Endorsements

There are many truths that when applied can be life changing. To know the truth will make you free—and all truth originates with the Word of God. Leon Gosiewski, and his revealing new book, 'Christianity Mis-sold', will take you on a step-by-step journey to see prophetically as mankind travels further and further away from God into the regions of darkness.

Along with the work Jesus called us to accomplish on His behalf—we literally die for it! Through years of proclaiming God's Word and His insight into the Scriptures, Leon Gosiewski, will both challenge and guide you in your walk to understanding God's unfailing mercy.

Read this book and continue to apply the principles contained within it and you will find freedom. Forever sealed in His love.

Apostle Dr. Theodore L. Dones
(D.Div. Th.D., Ph.D.)
International Circle of Faith College, Southern Indiana Bible College.

United Theological Seminary, TV Host of Messengers of Fire Ministries/ The Light TV Channel 21 WBNA, Founder of: Messengers of Fire Ministries and Five Fold Connection Magazine.

Author of Exposing the Secrets of the Heart.

My preparedness for being found "ready" has been a long, drawn out process, but your search can end today!

Sound biblical teaching, being hard to find, left me floundering, and searching out for myself, my journey into "holiness" – the prerequisite to my eternal destination. Oh that this book was given to me much sooner. My journey would have been so much the shorter, and sweeter, for having gleaned the glorious nutrients from its pages of content; right on into the "blessedness of the assurance", of the promises -- of the Truth and Wisdom of God.

My avenues of influence and instruction have varied greatly. Don't let that be your experience. You don't have "time" – time is running out; and fast! This book is all you need to realign you with your Redeemer and Lord, and His Holy Word; and your eternal right, (and necessity), to live a life of holiness – worthy of your calling in Christ Jesus; The same "call" that you will instantly recognise and respond to – Christianity Mis-sold! Amen!

'Remind [the people] of these facts and [solemnly] charge them in the presence of the Lord to avoid petty controversy over words, which does no good but upsets and undermines the faith of the hearers. Study and be eager and do your utmost to present yourself to God approved (tested by trial), a workman who has no cause to be ashamed, correctly analysing and accurately dividing [rightly handling and skilfully teaching] the Word of Truth.' (2 Timothy 2: 14, 15 Amplified Version)

This book will aid your beautiful, eternal journey, right on through the gates of glory, into the arms of your glorious God. One cannot share, what one does not possess. Brother Leon possesses, and here shares, in a true spirit of obedience and humility, the sacred teachings of the Word of God, for such a time as this – the end, of the end of days. He has "reminded us" and "rightly handled and skilfully taught" -- the Word of Truth; the same truth that has been missing from our churches for centuries.

The Trumpet will Sound – soon, and very soon. Are you ready

for that call? Will you recognise "it" and respond to "it"? This book will remove ALL doubt. You can only be blessed by its content, shared from the "holy heart" of a servant of the most High God! Be Blessed. I was! See you in Glory!

Leila Nord.
Founder and CEO of Jachin Boaz Ministries
Wellington NSW Australia

I have known Leon since 1976 and have always recognised his fervent love for Jesus. Leon's desire to stir faith in the people of God has always been evident and unquestionable.

Leon has a heart ablaze for God, burning with passion for the deeper, greater things that knowing, loving and serving God can bring, but so many of us fall short of. 'Christianity Mis-sold' will fan the flames of believers' hearts if you dare to accept the challenges that these pages hold.

God's word to Leon to 'Heal My Church' came as a clarion call to stir the people of God out of complacency into a sense of urgency in these end times. I believe Leon has captured exactly the urgency of the time and our need to be ready. Be prepared to be challenged.

Gwen Wills
Holly Road Elim Pentecostal Ladies Ministry, Hospital Chaplaincy and Aldershot Town Centre Pastoral Team Administrator.

This book seriously tested my Christian faith. James 1:3-4 says that: "...*the testing of our faith produces perseverance. Let perseverance finish its work so that you may be mature and complete, not lacking anything.*"

The most sincere endorsement I can give this book will be to heed its warning of urgency and put its words into action in my life. Leon swiftly makes it clear that the Kingdom of God is not for fence-sitters. It is an "in or out" Kingdom. Even if you call yourself a Christian you may find, (as I did), that your flesh, your complacency, your excuses for procrastination, your self-righteousness or any 'salvation through works' spirit in you will rail against this book. The key that will unlock its riches to you is genuine repentance. I swiftly found that I had to ask the Lord to forgive all my self-attitudes and replace them with a receptive spirit and discernment regarding the wisdom contained in these pages.

Here in this book lies the urgent truth to be embraced: "There is no room in the Kingdom of Heaven or in the life of a true believer for lethargy, complacency or procrastination. Where the Spirit of God dwells there is life, vibrancy, worship, truth, love and power." "*If the Spirit of God dwells in us then negativity and unbelief cannot co-exist.*" Deuteronomy 6:4-5 reminds us that "*The Lord our God, the Lord is one. Love the Lord your God with all your heart and with all your soul and with all your strength*". That's ... all ... all ... all - no division there...all and every part of us for God. Anything less is compromise and doesn't bring glory to Him - sadly when we compromise we devalue God's reputation and honour in the eyes of unbelievers. They miss His glory because we do not depict His glory in the Church Body.

The exhortation in this book is clear; the need to repent of all compromise is urgent but the rewards of obedience are vast gains for the Kingdom of God. Leon writes that "Repentance and forgiveness open a floodgate of love, reconciliation, peace, and harmony between us and God, God and us, us and others. It is also through repentance and forgiveness that the blood of Jesus covers us and the door of God's grace is opened wide." Leon's warning however is that anything less than this and we miss the narrow gate into the Kingdom of Heaven.

I commend this book to all who want their faith to be challenged, vibrant and true to God.

Paul Marriott
Workplace Christian Fellowship Co-Leader Christ Church, Roxeth.

'Now to him who by the power at work in us is able to do far more abundantly than all that we ask or think, to him be glory in the church and in Christ Jesus to all generations, for ever and ever. Amen.' 'I therefore, a prisoner for the Lord, beg you to lead a life worthy of the calling to which you have been called, with all lowliness and meekness, with patience, forbearing one another in love, eager to maintain the unity of the Spirit in the bond of peace. There is one body and one Spirit, just as you were called to the one hope that belongs to your call, one Lord, one faith, one baptism, One God and Father of us all, who is above all and through all and in all.' (Ephesians 3: 20 – 4: 6)

Contents

Acknowledgements

With heartfelt thanks to those nearest to my heart whom I love deeply and who in return love me, forgive me and show so much patience toward me.

Special thanks to my dear and lovely wife Chrissy.

Dedication

All glory and praise are given to God who has never failed me or forsaken me even though I have repeatedly failed Him. In thanks I offer myself as a living sacrifice.

The Foreword

When Leon invited me to write this foreword for 'Christianity Mis-sold' I felt honoured, but I also felt surprised, because fancy him sneaking off and writing another book! It explained why he had been a bit quiet lately. What had Leon and God been up to this time?

Let me tell you about the book, but if you hate reading forewords, let me simply say, 'buy the book'. You will receive a huge spiritual blessing from heaven if you do because doing so will also help you to hear God speaking to you, and it will definitely help you prepare for Christ's return.

'Christianity Mis-sold', is divided into seven chapters, each of which unpack key aspects that God has laid out for us in Scripture, to grow deeper, to please him more, to walk closer to him, to change more and more into his likeness, and to prepare so that we are fit and worthy to join him in heaven.

What God and Leon have worked on together in this book is essentially something very timely. This is a book for God's people living in the end of the end times. You could liken this book to a preparation manual for when the trumpet blast announces the arrival of Jesus, and we are up and away to join him, and not left, terror-struck! It is a very important book for everyone who wants to prepare for departure to join Christ at his imminent return.

Many believe that Christ's grace is our guarantee that we will definitely lead to being caught up with Christ, just as we are, no matter what. Many church leaders are encouraging people to believe this, but it is not what the Bible says! The Bible tells us to prepare and be ready! God and Leon have worked together to unpack biblical truth, and destroy dangerous myths.

I hope you find my chapter resume helpful:

Chapter 1 - 'To Him be glory in the church"

Leon begins by unpacking in its richness, why we are here and what we are to do while we are here. We are here to bring God glory. We bring God glory by bearing fruit. It is our fruit, our God-likeness showing God to the people around us that brings God glory. How we can do this best, is also contrasted against how we can do this worst! Our full submission, accompanied by our tears, driven by our love for God, is crucial in our journey to glorifying our God.

Chapter 2 - 'Transformation and renewal'

Digging deeper, Leon explores the necessary changes required in our thinking, changes made more difficult by so many churches that mirror worldly man, more than they do spiritual God. The way to renew the mind is through more Bible reading and knowledge. We must please God, not ourselves. We must not live sin, but live in righteousness; putting to death sin in our lives. Who we were before Christ, is clearly contrasted against who we are now that we are in Christ.

Chapter 3 - 'Repentance and forgiveness'

In this powerful and challenging chapter, Leon opens up the honest realities of being a repentant sinner, and keeping company with God. We can pretend repentance, which John the Baptist rebukes, using the famous phrase "brood of vipers" to those who looked repentant, but had no heart of regret and no fruits of repentance [Matthew 3:7-10]. Instead, we must turn away from our sin, our "idols" [Ezekiel 14:6]. Turning to forgiveness, Leon shows that it is not all about repentance and receiving forgiveness, but it is also essential that we forgive others [Matthew 6:14-15], because the forgiven live free, and in turn, must free others by forgiving them [Ephesians 4:29-32]. God requires that we are people of justice, love, mercy, and humility [Micah 6:8].

Chapter 4 - 'The grace of God'

Digging still deeper into fascinating territory, Leon now turns to grace, showing that the Good Shepherd puts the needs of the sheep ahead of his own needs - Christ died that we will live! Scripture says that Noah 'walked' with God, and found favour with Him [Genesis 6:9]. Leon points out that the Hebrew word for 'walk', means to 'follow, pursue, imitate, and live the same way of life.' When God went looking for the builder and captain of the Ark, he needed one who could hear him, one who would obey him, one who would see the task through and get the job done. It was a very important assignment; a rescue mission, a salvation mission, with some parallels to Christ's mission. In the life of Noah and in the life of Christ, we see active grace, favour, walking in God, and faith. God desires the same in our lives!

Chapter 5 - 'Living a life worthy of the calling'

Now Leon turns to living out the qualities of Christ. God desires harmony between his children, so that we function as one body under one head, Christ. As God has no division, nor must we. This means we are very careful about what we speak. Our words, our speech, have potential power for good or for bad. Our words can help to unify and harmonise our brothers and sisters, or our words can help hurt, splinter, and divide. What we express with our mouth should reflect lowliness, meekness, patience, and forbearance. Careless words are not the way of Christ [Matthew 12:36-37; 15:18-19].

Chapter 6 - 'Dare to live supernaturally'

This powerful and exciting chapter brings heaven's power supernatural to earth. Leon shows us, the church, how it is really meant to live; as it was in the first century; a church with supernatural power flowing from God. The supernatural life begins with us, and in us, with God choosing to reside in us [Isaiah 57:15]. Jesus, the vine and us the branches, is an analogy that implies the unique supernatural 'sap' that flows from Christ, making us supernaturally fruitful for His glory and for the blessing of God's people [John 15:5-8]. You will love this chapter. Leon dares you to live it...so does God.

Chapter 7 - 'Ready for the trumpet call'

The last assessment of ourselves...when the trumpet sounds, will we be found ready, or will we wish we had done more to prepare? Leon warns that Christ is coming at an hour we do not expect [Matthew 24:42-44], so we must always be ready for the Lord's arrival. God is testing us, disciplining us, and preparing us [Hebrews 12:5-6]. In fact, if we are not being disciplined and not ready for Christ's return, it is a sure sign that we are not children of God. Getting ready is one thing, but then we must stay ready, and staying ready cannot be separated from having God's high standard of love for others [1 John 3:14-15].

Conclusion

Leon concludes with reminders of the qualities God loves to see in you and in me, qualities that include 'doing justice, loving kindness and walking humbly with God' [Micah 6:8]. Leon encourages us to press on to know the Lord [Hosea 6:3]. We must prepare for the Lord's imminent return. Leon's 'Christianity Mis-sold', is a great preparation manual for being refined and ready to join our Lord in the clouds of heaven.

I hope my Foreword has blessed you and that you will buy this book and enjoy the manifold blessings I have enjoyed. I look forward to seeing you at the Wedding Feast. Save me a seat, Leon!

All glory to you our beautiful God.

David Dellit
God's scribe to The Valentine Prophecies and II Revelation

Preface

Christianity Mis-sold is a book birthed from an awesome encounter with Jesus that was so overwhelming that it left the author in uncontrollable tears and with the conviction of God's bleeding-heart for the renewal of His people before the door of opportunity and grace finally closes. The full impact and surprise of the meeting with Jesus came as the stark revelation of just how few are actually destined to enter the narrow gate to heaven. This was graphically revealed because most, who think they are securely in heaven, have in reality ill-prepared themselves for the Kingdom and have failed to live in Kingdom values. Jesus warned that not everyone who calls him Lord will enter heaven (Matthew 7:21)

This book poses the critical question, 'When the trumpet sounds will Jesus come for you or will you be left wishing you had walked according to the Spirit?' It provides clear Scripture-based answers that not only every believer should know, but which will transform hungry and thirsty lives for the Kingdom of God.

It is a book filled with God's love and longing to see you, His chosen and special child reach your full potential in Christ. It is also a book which brings the uncompromising discipline of a loving Father, who not only wants to prevent you from slipping along the path that leads to danger and harm, but who also knows how to set you straight - if only you will listen and act according to His warnings.

From a very early age, although I cannot tell you how or why, this one thought has not only rested firmly upon me but grown stronger as the years have passed; Jesus will return in my lifetime. This is not trying to predict a time or date, it is God's call upon me to stir the church, the true believers and followers of Jesus, into a deeper commitment and holy readiness.

Over the years I have not shared my conviction with many people. This is partly because I could not explain how a boy was thinking in this way, and partly because of the predictably dismissive response or the nonchalant quote that 'no-one knows' the timing.

During the last five years I have sensed an urgent intensity and increase toward the second coming of Jesus, which I believe is considerably closer than many realize. The tragedy of this prophetic statement is that many, like the maidens described in Matthew 25: 1 – 13 will foolishly not be equipped despite the very clear warning Jesus gave that we must constantly watch and be ready. (Matthew 24: 42 – 44)[1]

What countless people forget is that Jesus was the person who gave us the warning to watch and be ready. Sadly, over thousands of years, this is a warning that has lost its integrity because in a strange way many of us both see it and treat it a bit like the Aesop's fable, 'crying wolf', where a false alarm is given so many times people stop believing it. This has been particularly fuelled by those over the centuries who have been cunningly set in place by our evil adversary to predict a particular day and month when the world will end. The fact is, we certainly do not know the specific day or time. But what has been lost in all of this confusion is the fact that God has and will use clear warning signs that point directly to the second coming. And so, whoever you are, both you and I have a personal responsibility not only to heed the warnings but to be obedient in doing so.

---

1   Matthew 24: 42 – 44 – 'Watch therefore, for you do not know on what day your Lord is coming. But know this, that if the householder had known in what part of the night the thief was coming, he would have watched and would not have let his house be broken into.' Our duty is to keep watching and continue in a state of constant alertness and readiness.

About four years ago God laid on my heart the need for His Church to be healed. At first I did not understand the message but, what I now know is the strength of leading to announce that we must get ready, walk in the Spirit and be fully equipped, because when that trumpet sound is heard, it will be too late to put everything right with the Lord who is returning for those whom we read in Ephesians 5: 27 are without spot or blemish.

The Old Testament prophet Ezekiel was given this message:

'If I bring the sword upon a land, and the people of the land take a man from among them, and make him their watchman; and if he sees the sword coming upon the land and blows the trumpet and warns the people; then if any one who hears the sound of the trumpet does not take warning, and the sword comes and takes him away, his blood shall be upon his own head.' (Ezekiel 33: 2 – 4)

I believe we are in the last of the last days. There are increasing numbers of God's watchmen across the globe sounding the trumpet and warning people. The sword of God is coming. Tragically, there are many in the church today that instead of listening and acting upon what they hear – target the watchmen instead by shooting arrows to silence them. Arrows of complacency, criticism, disbelief and verbal abuse are used to silence and isolate the watchmen. This is tragic because for those who hear the trumpet sound of the watchman and release their arrows of disregard, God makes an awesome, spine-chilling and clear statement in Ezekiel 33: 4 that this person's **'blood shall be upon his own head.'**

Many watchmen throughout Scripture, and even in the church today, have been abysmally treated and have suffered at the hands of those hurling criticism and ill-treatment. But God says to the watchman, if he fails to sound the trumpet, not only will the people be taken away in their sin but their blood will eventually be required at the watchman's hands! (Ezekiel 33: 6)[2]

---

2   Ezekiel 33: 6 – *'But if the watchman sees the sword coming and does not blow the trumpet, so that the people are not warned, and the sword comes, and takes any one of them; that man is taken away in his iniquity, but his blood I will require at the watchman's hand.'*

'Christianity Mis-sold' is a watchman's call to not only do whatever is personally required to get fully prepared and ready, but also, to reach out and save the lost. You see, what we must realize is that every Christian believer is personally required to faithfully be an ambassador of Jesus Christ. And, as Christ's ambassador, our job is to tangibly bring Heaven to earth.

The countdown clock is ticking and it is time to stop simply praying 'Your will be done on earth as it is in Heaven' and actually do it. We are not only the channels of Heaven on earth, but because of Jesus the Kingdom of Heaven is within us. That is why John boldly declared, *'he who is in you is greater than he who is in the world'* (1 John 4:4)

The 'how' is what this book is all about. The, 'what must I do' is at the core of each chapter. The means is you and me. The glory is God made manifest.

Prologue

Paul made an awesome point when he left this open question containing cautionary doubt, *'if indeed the Spirit of God dwells in you'* (Romans 8:9)

I am constantly amazed by the lethargic reaction of Christian believers who pay little attention or even simply ignore statements like Paul's found in Scripture. There is a prevalent blasé attitude that skips past these types of uncomfortable and directly challenging statements or questions, which breed a false sense of security and hope; a false security and hope, which leads to a costly and negative spiritual life of lethargy, complacency and procrastination.

If the Spirit of God reigns supreme on the throne of our heart, negativity and unbelief will be removed. But what every Christian believer must know and understand is that Scripture is full of examples of both various tests being applied to believers and wise exhortations that encourage us to constantly scrutinize ourselves and stay faithfully alert. For example:

- God left Hezekiah to try or test him (2 Chronicles 32: 31)
- Jesus tested Philip to see what he would say and do (John 6: 6)
- Paul encouraged us to test ourselves (2 Corinthians 13: 5)

- Paul also encourages us to examine ourselves
  (1 Corinthians 9: 27, 11: 28 and 2 Corinthians 13: 5)
- The testing of our faith produces steadfastness (James 1: 3)

James explains why the testing of our faith is so important. It is because it produces steadfastness, commitment, dedication and endurance so that, as James put it *'you may be perfect and complete, lacking in nothing.'* (James 1: 4)

No Christian believer can simply sit back and ride on someone else's anointing, ministry or blessing. None of us can rely on past spiritual success or blessing. We cannot simply say I came to Jesus and so I am okay. Paul made these points clear when he said, *'forgetting what lies behind and straining forward to what lies ahead, I press on toward the goal for the prize of the upward call of God in Christ Jesus'* (Philippians 3: 13, 14). It is not who we were or what we did yesterday. It is who we are and what we do today!

The truth is that there is no room in the Kingdom of Heaven or in the life of a true believer for lethargy, complacency or procrastination. Where the Spirit of God dwells there is life, vibrancy, worship, truth, love and power. There is no standing still as daily we move from one degree of glory to the next.

Paul wrote: *'that if possible I may attain the resurrection from the dead. Not that I have already obtained this or am already perfect; but I press on to make it my own, because Christ Jesus has made me his own'* (Philippians 3: 11 – 12) and *'I do not run aimlessly, I do not box as one beating the air; but I pommel my body and subdue it, lest after preaching to others I myself should be disqualified'* (1 Corinthians 9: 26, 27). Dear reader, whatever you may have heard beforehand know this from God's word, the journey is not ended until we reach the end and squeeze through the narrow gate and into the kingdom of heaven.

The Kingdom of Heaven which Jesus spoke of is an in-or-out Kingdom. If we are not totally in the Kingdom we are totally outside it, there is no fence-sitting. It is an entire commitment that starts when we nail our lives to the cross of Calvary, dying to self and leaving it on the cross. This is why the true believer cannot be of the world or flesh!

There are many Christian believers walking a 'tight-rope' fraught with dangers that they actually do not need to walk. The 'tight-rope' is called worldly living, which lacks commitment and dedication. The path to Heaven is hard enough without making it almost, if not completely impossible to sustain.

'Christianity Mis-sold' is about making sure that as Christian believers we know exactly what is expected of us, what we must do and how we can - and must - support one another as we look to the coming of our precious Lord and Saviour Jesus Christ.

Chapter One

To Him Be Glory in the Church

'Now to him who by the power at work in us is able to do far more abundantly than all that we ask or think, to him be glory in the church and in Christ Jesus to all generations, for ever and ever. Amen.' (Ephesians 3: 20, 21)

In one way or another we all hold opinions about a variety of matters, situations and circumstances that we come across in our daily life. From these we make judgments based upon what we see and experience. Our view of a person, an organization or even belief system is influenced and weighed by the opinions we build and the consequent decisions we make.

This continuous process is necessary for all of us as part of our every-day living and helps us to make informed choices. For example, where we experience bad, unsavoury or conflicting things or where we come across people's poor attitudes, we act according to these discoveries to avoid connection. And of course, if the resulting evidence of what we experience is good and those we meet make a positive impact, we are magnetically drawn and attracted toward them.

All of this is not only true of life in general but also of our personal view of the church, and crucially how the world looking in from the outside not only judges it, but judges each of us individually as its members. With this thought in mind, Paul wrote these powerful words, *'to him be glory in the church'* (Ephesians 3: 21). But what exactly did Paul mean in this statement?

Let's begin by looking at the opening key words of Ephesians 3: 21 which say *'to him.'* Here our attention is specifically drawn toward God. The focus of our consideration is God and when we read the rest of the sentence this becomes clearer because it says, *'to him be glory in the church and in Christ Jesus to all generations.'* The emphasis is upon honouring God and bringing glory to His name in the church. To put this in another way, it is the spiritual responsibility of the church to radiate the glory of God into the world.

The depth and meaningful impact of what Paul wrote to the Ephesian church becomes even clearer when we as Christian believers realize that it is God whom we represent, and it is our holy responsibility to personify this both as a body of believers and in our personal lives to all humankind, whether they are within or outside the church.

To put what I have said in another way, how we represent the church, not only toward one another but to the world is important because we are the face of God. I really cannot stress this point too strongly. It is vitally important that each one of us as true believers and followers of Christ fully grasp and understand the tremendous holy duty and accountability laid upon us to bring glory to God through the church. This is a weight of responsibility that none of us, whoever we are, whatever place or title we may or may not have in our churches can shirk or side-step. We are all in it together as God's holy light-bearers!

The plain fact is this; if we do not shine the light of Jesus and walk under the anointed power of the Holy Spirit we are not bringing glory to God. This fact was as true when Paul wrote it as it is for each of us today because Paul covered and emphasized this point when he wrote, *'to all generations.'* In other words, what we mirror in and through our lives also has a perpetual influence on those both immediately around us and how they pass that down from one generation to another. The church in the past, present and the future has had and continues to have, the same responsibility.

In fact, the vital importance of rightly informing the world about God and bringing glory to His name is something the Old Testament prophet Habakkuk discovered in his soliloquy with God. He asked about the seeming injustice that the wicked give the impression of having the advantage over the just and go unpunished. But God made this point; the wicked will not prosper and avoid His judgement and this will be a fact made plainly known to everyone because, *'the earth will be filled with the knowledge of the glory of the Lord'* (Habakkuk 2: 14). You see when we commit our lives to God, we not only become His appointed carriers and examples of His message but we must also fulfil His intention to fill the earth with the knowledge of His glory. But there is more; because as carriers and examples of God's messages, we are duty bound to do this rightly! That means we must know what is right!

It suddenly becomes clear from these opening Scripture discoveries, that God has faithfully placed a great onus upon the church and yet, it remains an onus that has tragically neither been meaningfully understood nor acted upon. It has instead become a perpetual failing of the church that neither individually nor collectively we can afford to allow to continue because, although we might think we have escaped our duties, God will bring His judgement. We will be called to give our account.

Since each believer must allow the holiness of God to rein in their life, it is imperative that we fully understand what the term glory really means, therefore let's take a closer look at this important word.

Glory in the Church

The word glory used in the context of Ephesians chapter three is the Greek word ***doxa***, which literally refers to the opinion, judgment and view that people hold of the Father, Son and Holy Spirit, and of course, as members of the church, each one of us. The Hebrew word for glory is ***kabowd***, a word that sharpens the Greek meaning of doxa because it refers specifically to God's reputation and honour. That means each of us has the task of preserving God's reputation through the life we live. Yes, you did read that correctly and it is for that reason it is worth repeating that, each of us, both you and me has the task of preserving God's reputation through the life we live. The world should be attracted to the light and love of Jesus in us and not be distracted by our worldliness.

If the realization that we are guardians of God's reputation does not bring us humbly to our knees something is terribly wrong in our relationship with God. Why do I say this? Well, it is because if we are to guard the precious reputation of God in our lives we must bring Him in our bodily form to earth. Listen to what Isaiah wrote, *'For thus says the high and lofty One who inhabits eternity, whose name is Holy: 'I dwell in the high and holy place, and also with him who is of a contrite and humble spirit, to revive the spirit of the humble, and revive the heart of the contrite'* (Isaiah 57: 15). In these few words Isaiah reaches into the heart of our relationship with God, which flourishes if we have a humble and contrite spirit because then God dwells with us, His Spirit is upon us. When God's Spirit is upon us it revives us. Now when we look at the Hebrew word for revive used here we discover the word **chayah** which means to quicken, bring alive or enliven. In other words, there is nothing dull or spiritually dead in us; we cannot help but glow with the life, love and power of God.

Did you grasp that amazing last point? If God is truly in us, we are filled to overflowing with His love and power. His Spirit enlivens us to such an extent that we cannot help but show His presence, love and power. We cannot be devoid of spiritual liveliness, love and supernatural power!

Jesus plainly told us exactly how we bring glory to His Father, *'that you bear much fruit, and so prove to be my disciples'* (John 15: 8). In other words, if we are not bearing abundant Kingdom fruit in our lives we are not bringing glory to God. In fact we are also not proving our discipleship!

Interestingly, the Greek word for prove used in John 15: 8 is **ginomai**, which means to come into existence, become, turn into or to receive. In other words, it is when we bear fruit that we become or receive the recognition as true disciples.

You see, bringing glory to God is all about the attractive and exuding wonder, splendour and admiration that people will see and feel toward God because He radiates like the heat of a fire from us. It is all about how we as humble servants conduct ourselves and to what extent the life and power of Jesus is at work in and through us that people will both view and judge the church. But more than this, it is how they may view the Creator God we represent.

I wonder, how many times you have heard people outside the church justifiably say those Christians are no better; they say one thing and do something else? Look at the scandals of child abuse in some churches. Look at how one Christian criticises another or one church disagrees with another. Yes, praise God exceptions and good things exist in some of our churches, but these get clouded and outweighed by the bad things. When the world looks at the church it can see too much of society and secular entertainment sandwiched between hymns and prayers with ministers even taking courses on how to tell jokes so that they can keep the interest of the gathered people - this will never bring the power of God. If the Lord's presence is not glowing from within, no number of jokes will hold people's attention and the power of God will certainly never be seen.

Even where good sermons and teachings are faithfully delivered how many churches immediately engage in worldly concerns and gossip over tea and biscuits only to lose not just the impact but the practical outworking delivered in the meeting!

Beneath our noses, the social distraction of tea, cake and biscuits can and sadly often are tools of satan designed to weaken our relationship with God and with each other. There is too much church focus that is pally with society and humanism instead of separating itself and walking in holiness. If we truly want to make an impact on the gospel message we must allow it to live through us until we become it. If it is necessary, let's sup tea, drink coffee and eat cake to the glory of God by showing true hospitality; meeting the needs of the saints with love, serving one another and sharing with the poor and needy as we put the gospel message into practise and not talk about worldly matters.

If we show lack of love toward one another, disharmony, criticism and poor standards of behaviour and attitudes people will understandably turn their backs both on us and any aspiration to know God. They will see that we are no better than those they experience in the world around them and also, that we say one thing in a holy huddle and then live in a totally different and worldly way; indistinguishable from any other person. Furthermore that we make claims that we cannot show the reality and truth of. The spiritual dullness or lifelessness in us will show a dull or lifeless church.

Of course, we might think we are okay looking from our inner cosy perspective, but we fool ourselves if we think the world looking in at the church from the outside does not see its spiritual credentials. People have a God-shaped hole in their lives. They are seeking the love, honesty and integrity of Jesus. They are looking for the real God to step forward and show Himself. They know the world is not enough. We are the face of God. He has chosen us to represent Him through Jesus, the Head of the church.

Whatever you may think of what I have said so far the question we must ask ourselves is, 'can we honestly say we are the church of our Lord and Saviour Jesus Christ and living as He taught'? Our obligation is to honestly admit and purposely do something about the truth that the church has lost its way and it is not what it should truly be because it has lost its first love. It is not the church Jesus came to build because it has loosened its roots and teachings. Churches have become a place of disparate denominations created by man instead of Jesus. It has become a church led by man and not the Holy Spirit. It has become a church that preaches man's doctrines - not God's. It has become a church that demands soft, flattering and unchallenging messages with promises of personal gain and prosperity instead of separation from the world and worldly desires.

We must face the fact that there is literally no hiding place from God. The church has for far too long been guilty of lowering its standards and attempting to duplicate society, humanism, watered down gospel messages and a belief that does not show the love and light of Jesus or the anointed power of the Holy Spirit at work in us.

If we are going to see God move among us with a release of the fire of the Holy Spirit this must not continue. The state of the church and therefore each one of us must change and improve in line with God's will and in honour of our blessed Lord and Saviour Jesus Christ. I do not mean any of this uncharitably but it is time for each of us to wake up, get up and do something about the situation that we have fallen into; the discredit instead of credit that we have brought to God.

Think about it. How do we react if someone hurts a member of our family or a close friend? Do we stand and watch and do nothing? No! Because we love them so deeply we come to their defence and we do what we can to help, support and rebuild the damage caused. Yet when it comes to our beloved Jesus how many times have we remained silent? How many times have we stood back and done nothing? How many times have we been motivated to actually change ourselves and put Jesus first?

You see, just as any company or organization that has been found guilty of malpractice and wrongdoing must work hard to change its appearance and improve standards to regain customer confidence or it will fold and die, likewise the church and each of us individually must improve the standards of who we are as the church and walk in the Spirit and holiness of God to create our true identity. It is up to us to change what is happening in our churches.

The bottomline is this; I believe Jesus is coming for His church and it will be very soon. Scripture is clear about this fact. He is coming for those within the church that are, *'without spot or wrinkle or any such thing, that she might be holy and without blemish'* (Ephesians 5: 27). If any of us fail to safeguard that we are without spot, wrinkle or blemish we will not only be found lacking in our duty to bring glory to God but we will also miss the mark required of those Jesus is returning for and be left behind!

Scripture already warns us of the outcome of failing churches. The second and third chapters of the New Testament book of Revelation are absolutely clear. We have no excuse because it has already been graphically revealed to John and recorded for each of us to plainly see what God has against many churches and how they will eventually be judged:

- Ephesus had fallen from its first love (Revelation 2: 4)
- Pergamum taught things that were contrary to God's word (Revelation 2: 14, 15)
- Thyatira allowed outside influences that led to the teaching of immoral things (Revelation 2: 20)
- Sardis had the outward appearance of being alive but were actually dead and displeasing to God (Revelation 3: 1 – 3)
- Laodicea a complacent church was neither one thing or the other (Revelation 3: 15 – 17)

It is frightening to read these Scripture revelations and then look at the state and condition of churches today. How many have fallen from their first love and now the life and vibrancy of the Lord is missing? How many are teaching things that are contrary to Scripture - such as all you need to do is say a prayer and you are immediately saved with no more requirements, or teachings that say it is not always God's will to heal? How many churches are so extensively influenced by society that they allow and even teach and embrace immorality such as naturist churches and same-sex marriages? How many churches look okay but little or nothing of the power of God actually exists? They say the right things but do not act on them and live the truth, displeasing God in the process. How many churches are complacent, content and happy so long as no one 'rocks the boat' and challenges them? How many churches will miss the point completely and say, 'we are not perfect but we are seeing some good things happening' and take no further action?

As we have discovered from the message to the seven churches found in Revelation 2: 1 – 3: 22, five of the seven churches were found inadequate even though some good things were obviously recognized and acknowledged. Tragically many churches today find themselves among the five churches of Revelation. Many will be judged by God in exactly the same way. But by the incredible love and grace of God we also read something remarkable; a life-line thrown to the churches and each one of us individually that we would be foolish to the extreme to ignore or reject:

- Ephesus was painstakingly reminded to – *'Remember then from what you have fallen, repent and do the works you did at first'* (v5)

- Pergamum was sternly encouraged to – *'Repent then'* (v16)
- Thyatira was lovingly reminded to – *'hold fast what you have'* (v25)
- Sardis was given instruction to – *'Remember then what you received and heard; keep that, and repent'* (v3)
- Laodicea was passionately stirred to – *'be zealous and repent'* (v19)

The opportunity to get back on track and repent is with the church, before it is too late, but it comes with the proviso that we must conquer:

'To him who conquers – (this is the key; we must see everything through to the end and triumphantly conquer, and then we will receive these promises):

- *'I will grant to eat of the tree of life, which is in the paradise of God'* (Revelation 2: 7)
- *'shall not be hurt by the second death'* (Revelation 2: 11)
- *'I will give some of the hidden manna, and I will give him a white stone, with a new name written on the stone which no one knows except him who receives it'* (Revelation 2: 17)
- *'I will give him power over the nations, and he shall rule them with a rod of iron, as when earthen pots are broken in pieces, even as I myself have received power from my Father: and I will give him the morning star'* (Revelation 2: 26 – 28)
- *'shall be thus clad in white garments, and I will not blot his name out of the book of life; I will confess his name before my Father and before his angels'* (Revelation 3: 5)
- *'I will make him a pillar in the temple of my God; never shall he go out of it, and I will write on him the name of my God, and the name of the city of my God, the new Jerusalem which comes down from my God out of heaven, and my own new name'* (Revelation 3: 12)
- *'I will grant him to sit with me on my throne, as I myself conquered and sat down with my father on his throne'* (Revelation 3: 21)

The church must work with submissive determination to conquer. Time and again in Scripture we are clearly told that we must repent and do the works that Jesus did by zealously holding and keeping God's word. Repeatedly we are reminded in these revelatory Scriptures that it is '*he who conquers*' that will receive the promised prize. This all brings us to an important crunch-point; one that may challenge some reading this to the core of not only what bringing glory to God and the church is all about but what being a Christian believer really means. The fact is, if we are not bringing glory to the church we are not living the Christian life that Jesus died on the cross for and to which God has called us; but why? What has happened? Why aren't we living the Christian life as it should be lived?

The problem that originally led to the downward spiral of the church lies partly in the fact that it stopped its tenacious teaching of scriptural truth. The church lost its first love of Jesus and what being a Christian believer really means. It allowed man to control its direction, thoughts and teaching. It has, in our modern-day parlance, mis-sold the requirements of being a true believer in a raft of watered-down messages and man-inspired ideals, many of which now bear little resemblance to the true heart of Scripture.

Christianity Mis-sold

To illustrate my point you will know as well as I do that mis-selling is unfortunately a common feature in the world brought about by dishonest practice that puts a person or company at an advantage over the unsuspecting. Many of us have sadly been caught out by the cleverly deceptive lure of mis-selling tactics.

Some of us eventually realize they have been mis-sold and actively do something about it to regain what they have lost whilst others, although they come to know they have been cleverly deceived, do nothing. Perhaps worse still are those who have been mis-sold but who do not realize the trickery and so they carry on in that misguided and costly belief.

Of course, mis-selling in the world is one thing and it can and has brought great hurt, pain and loss. Mis-selling in the churches however is not only the cause of great hurt and pain, it can lead to disastrous eternal outcomes.

Christianity has been mis-sold as a belief that excuses our sinful weaknesses and requires little effort or dedication. It is falsely sold as a belief that takes the benefits but requires no real effort and anguish; a belief that we can talk about but not live in its true essence every day. The mis-selling of the Christian walk has caused many to think they are okay when in reality they are not. They think the bare minimum of effort and commitment is enough.

Our adversary, the devil has been at work in churches[3] since the beginning and despite the warnings and efforts of the early church founders and leaders, many following generation after generation have been subtly deceived and bit-by-bit, thrown off course or lured by egotistical benefits.

Just as an army in combat will seek to infiltrate and cut off the life-line of an enemy, so in spiritual warfare that is what the devil has done. It is a tragic fact that the requirements of a Christian walk have commonly been so diluted that it does not teach or explain it either correctly or in adequate detail. This is the case even though the Bible is clear and hides nothing. Many, as a direct result have become blinded to the true costs of total commitment, repentance, holiness, taking up our cross, walking with God, growing daily and laying down our lives. Yes, we have heard about them, but the depth of the commitment has not been adequately emphasized and realized. It gets mashed-up with talk about God's love and grace, important though these are, but they are convincingly expressed to such an extent that we become desensitized and even complacent.

---

3   Ephesians 6: 11 – *'Put on the whole armor of God, that you may be able to stand against the wiles of the devil.'*
Galatians 3: 1 – *'O foolish Galatians! Who has bewitched you, before whose eyes Jesus Christ was publicly portrayed as crucified?'*

The Fallacy of Belief

The modern message that all we need to do is believe in Jesus, say a prayer and everything is okay is nothing short of a lie of the devil. Man has completely stripped the biblical word believe of its real meaning.

Oh yes, we talk about believing in Jesus but we often do so at a superficial level. James gave an example of this superficiality when he said, *'You believe that God is one; you do well. Even the demons believe – and shudder'* (James 2: 19). Clearly, to simply believe is not enough. Even the demons believe but actually they do something many of us do not do, they shudder! Something therefore goes beyond just believing.

For example, I believe Queen Victoria lived but I do not know her any more than I know Queen Elizabeth II. I can read as much as I like about her, but I will never know her, the person. I also believe I have over twenty-two feet of intestine in my body but I am never going to find out and know the exact length. Can you see that to simply believe in someone or something is not enough? I hope you can grasp that to believe in Jesus the man is one thing, to know Him and know that you know is quite different. It is a revelation knowledge that Jesus expressed in this way, that a person *'does not doubt in his heart, but believes'* (Mark 11: 23). This belief moves from a simple feeling or head knowledge belief to a knowing heart knowledge belief. Any element of doubt or of not knowing Jesus is totally removed because He is alive and we can walk and talk with Him. It is a relationship that grows and draws us closer as we get to know His heart, see through His eyes, know His personality and so believe to such an extent that there is no doubt. It is about a meeting with the living Jesus that comes as we reach out to Him. Most often this life-changing encounter comes through the life-glowing introduction of those that represent Him in their lives and through what they say and do.

Our integrity in presenting the truth about Jesus is important. Sadly what many are not told is that sin leads us to death but so does giving one's life to God and Jesus! Avoiding death in this sense is not possible for anyone. 'Whoa, hang on' you might say. 'That's a bit strong and over the top.' Please let me explain. We know from Scriptures such as Isaiah 59: 2[4], that sin separates us from God and when we go to the grave with sin unresolved and unforgiven, it leads to eternal spiritual death in hell, with separation from God not only continued but made permanent. If sin is the cause of separating us from God it must surely make sense that we should separate ourselves from it.

Separating ourselves from sin begins when we give our lives to Jesus. The first step is taken when we choose before the grave to resolve sin issues in our lives and die spiritually to self. In other words, we readily choose to give ourselves totally to God and that means we willingly cease self-ownership, we hand all self-will, self-direction and self-attitudes to Jesus, not only as our Saviour but as Lord. In other words we become His bond-servants because He has purchased us by His blood on the cross of Calvary (1 Corinthians 6: 19, 20)[5]. When we physically die the selfless bond with our Lord is continued and we permanently reside with Him in heaven.

What I have said so far may be new and uncompromising to some readers. They are spoken from a heart of love and desire to remain true to Scripture. It is in this regard that I will not mis-sell the total and absolute dedicated requirement and obligation to Jesus that means death to self. The plain truth is there is no shortcut route to Heaven for anyone which is why Jesus said, *'strive to enter by the narrow door; for many, I tell you, will seek to enter and will not be able'* (Luke 13: 24). There have never been promises in Scripture that life will suddenly get easy. The path to the Kingdom of God has never been painted in Scripture by any other way than, *'many, I tell you, will seek to enter and will not be able.'* Jesus honestly and openly said, *'if any man would come after me, let him deny himself and take up his cross and follow me. For whoever would save his life will lose it, and whoever loses his life for my sake will find it'* (Matthew 16: 24, 25).

---

4   Isaiah 59: 2 – *'But your iniquities have made a separation between you and your God, and your sins have hid his face from you so that he does not hear.'*
5   1 Corinthians 6: 19, 20 – *'Do you not know that your body is a temple of the Holy Spirit within you, which you have from God? You are not your own; you were bought with a price. So glorify God in your body.'*

The personal choice for each one of us is either to physically live life on earth in sin and separated from God, die and spend eternity in hell separated from Him - or spiritually die to our own interests on earth; connect with God through Jesus, physically die and spend eternity in Heaven joined with Him. There is no middle ground, it is all or nothing. Therefore it makes sense that we fully understand the journey to the narrow gate.

The Narrow Gate

Let's begin building our understanding of the narrow gate by reminding ourselves what Jesus said, *'Enter by the narrow gate; for the gate is wide and the way easy, that leads to destruction, and those who enter by it are many. For the gate is narrow and the way is hard, that leads to life, and those who find it are few'* (Matthew 7: 13, 14). In these concise words we are pictorially and honestly told that the gate or door that leads to Heaven is small and narrow. In other words, even for those that reach this far in the journey, it is still a squeeze to get through it! But more than this, the holy integrity of Scripture tells us that the path or road to this door is hard or some Bible translations say narrow. The descriptive Greek word for narrow used here is **thlibo**, which means affliction, tribulation, trouble or being so weighed down that it is as if being pressed like grapes to extract the juices. What an apt picture of our journey to Heaven the crushing of grapes paints. There are times in our spiritual life journey where everything seems to press against us, squeezing everything out of us until all we have left is our faith to hang on to.

There are also times when God seems to disappear, or hide himself. This is a characteristic of God that once we understand his purpose, will change us. For example:

- God left Hezekiah to try or test him (2 Chronicles 32: 31)
- Isaiah actually said that God hides Himself (Isaiah 45: 15)
- Jesus tested Philip to see what he would say and do (John 6: 6)

Job experienced a feeling that he could not find God when he said, *'Behold, I go forward, but he is not there; and backward, but I cannot perceive him; on the left hand I seek him, but I cannot behold him; I turn to the right hand, but I cannot see him'* (Job 23: 8, 9). Job was thrown to his faith and trust in God; he did not give up, knowing that what he faced was a test of his commitment and so he was able to say, *'But he knows the way that I take; when he has tried me, I shall come forth as gold. My foot has held fast to his steps; I have kept his way and have not turned aside. I have not departed from the commandments of his lips; I have treasured in my bosom the words of his mouth.'* (Job 23: 10 – 12)

The point Jesus was also making is that there is nothing easy about entering the Kingdom of God and so someone that suddenly realized what Jesus was saying asked this logical and pertinent question, **'Lord, will those who are saved be few?'** And He said to them, *'Strive to enter by the narrow door; for many, I tell you, will seek to enter and will not be able'* (Luke 13: 23, 24). Wow, what a shocking statement. Jesus gave the straightforward answer; we have to strive, we will be tested and it will be what we might call today, a slog to enter the Kingdom of Heaven because many will try but fail!

Interestingly the Greek work for strive used by Jesus is **Agonizomai** meaning to contend, fight or zealously work at. Some confuse striving or working hard to enter the kingdom by saying, 'It is by faith and God's grace that we are saved.' Although this is true in essence, it is not an excuse to sit back and do little or nothing to keep ourselves on the narrow path.

This message was crushingly brought home to me one day whilst I was out walking and talking with Jesus. He showed me just *how few* this Scripture really means. And I can tell you it has left such a mark that it causes me to share with as many as possible the urgent message to wake-up and not rely on what man has taught about salvation.

What was about to happen took me by surprise when Jesus led me to a local graveyard where I could see hundreds upon hundreds of gravestones. I sat quietly for a while pondering how many in these graves had not heard the gospel message. And how many who heard the gospel message had not been taught the truths of it. Out of curiosity, I asked Jesus how many in the graveyard were in Heaven. He told me to step forward along the first path that separated the rows of gravestones. I had not gone far along the path before He told me to stop. The distance was only three lines. I turned to look at the three lines and cast my eyes across the entire width of the graveyard only to find myself totally stunned when Jesus said 'no' and He directed me to look to my right. I estimated that the area He showed me was about one percent of the graveyard. In total shock I pleaded that this could not be right and I questioned what Jesus had shown me. Surely, I had mistaken what I had seen? But when Jesus confirmed what He had revealed to me, I cried uncontrollably.

Still shocked by what I had been shown, a few weeks later I asked Jesus about this hard and narrow road. He showed me that the road is treacherous and slippery. It is why we find ourselves slipping backward or what we generally and without really knowing it accurately call, backsliding.

The Lord also showed me that there are side paths, like slides. Many people enter these, some slide back to a lower part of the road and then begin the climb again. Some of these people constantly slip back and make no real headway. Others slide off the road completely, never to return. The shocking thing about this, are the numbers that do not even make it to the gate. They have either fallen off the path completely or they are fixed on it, unable to actually enter the gate.

Some people however discover how to negotiate the difficult road; they realize that it cannot be conquered without help and use of the correct tools. The picture I saw was similar to a mountaineer using equipment such as a harness, ropes, crampons and karabiners. The message I received was that we must do the same in our spiritual climb to heaven. We must use the right guide, equipment and tenacity to keep the faith.

We need:

- The harness of total submission that allows us to hold on to and rely on God

- The rope firmly attached to Jesus
- The crampons of the Holy Spirit attached to our shoes to keep our feet firm and on the path
- The karabiners of faith firmly placed into the rock to keep us from falling away when things get tough.

The point is that no mountaineer would ever attempt to climb a rock face before understanding the task, choosing the right partner and guide and fully equipping themselves. So we must do the same in our spiritual climb to Heaven. The ill-equipped, untrained, complacent and spiritually unfit never make the journey because they are not suitably attired, equipped and obediently focused on their guide.

Christianity has too often been mis-sold as simply "believe in Jesus" but there is nothing about the true cost; nothing about the total commitment and nothing about the true meaning of dying to self. In reality the Christian life is a daily walk, a progressive journey, moving from one place of our walk to another guided by the Holy Spirit every day.

There is no small print or hidden requirements to the Christian life in the Bible. Only man has missed the entire message and passed these on as a watered down requisite. No wonder the church is impotent and losing not just precious souls but also God's favour.

If the truth that Jesus said "many will try to enter the Kingdom but fail" does not cause us to urgently do something to test ourselves and make sure we measure up, perhaps nothing ever will. We will be like those that realize all is not well and yet still sit back and do nothing.

What I hope is gained from this chapter, is that readers will realize the importance of total commitment and obedience to God, repent and walk in total dedication to Jesus for the rest of their lives. I hope and pray that churches will discover the keys to living the Christian life as God intends and fulfil their obligation to bring God glory in the church.

Finding the Keys

Talking of keys, we are all familiar with the use of keys of one type or another. We will all also have quickly discovered that although a key is a means of unlocking something to gain access or to divulge what is behind the door or lid, only the correct key for the lock will allow entry. Of course, even having the correct key for the lock means that we must not only place it into the lock the right way up but we have to actually use it by physically turning it.

Assuming the lock is in good working order, the door or lid will open if the the correct key is used. In the Christian life, the Bible is our door lock to the Kingdom of Heaven. There is nothing wrong with the Bible but we do have to use the right keys in the right way. There is an action obligation placed upon us before we can gain access to the help and promises that lie behind the door of Scripture.

Reading the Bible alone will have little effect if we do not actually use the keys provided to physically, spiritually and mentally unlock the treasures within.

Finding the correct key for different situations and circumstances takes dedication to the Word and the precious help of the Holy Spirit. We will have to sift through the keys to find the right one for the purpose. That is why walking in the holy illumination of the Holy Spirit and truth of the Word of God, or as Scripture puts it, walking in spirit and truth is so important in these last of the last days.

We are totally finished with the days where preaching the truth of Scripture alone is enough. We are also finished with the days when walking in the spirit alone is enough. These are the days of truth and spirit. These are the days where truth and spirit are snugly joined like a hand enclosed by a good fitting glove.

As we have discovered, contrary to some man-inspired teaching there are no easy paths in the Christian walk that lead to the Kingdom. We cannot sit back, with our feet up and hope everything will be okay. Lethargy, complacency and procrastination have no room in the Christian walk because there is no lethargy, complacency or procrastination in God. These are the days where with holy tears and anguish we have to hunger and thirst for God. But, having said this, where are the tears and anguish today?

Holy Tears

When Nehemiah heard about the sacrilegious destruction of the Holy Temple in Jerusalem, the surrounding city and dispersion of the Jewish people he said, *'I sat down and wept, and mourned for days; and I continued fasting and praying before the God of heaven'* (Nehemiah 1: 4). Nehemiah did not blame God or attempt to find excuses or answers to satisfy his grief over what had happened. Nehemiah took responsibility for what had occurred and in an act of humble and contrite repentance confessed both his and the sins of the Jewish people committed against God.

For many of us the Christian faith has been so watered down that we do not fully understand the finer nuances and significance of our sin against God. We seem to have forgotten the words of Paul who said, *'Do you not know that your body is a temple of the Holy Spirit within you, which you have from God?'* (1 Corinthians 6: 19). Since our body is a temple of the Holy Spirit, our sin and disobedience bring destruction to our temple, and a direct result of this is exactly what the Jewish people experienced: dispersion, separation and loss of God's fullness in us and with us.

Generally speaking, we are not grieved by the rapid and growing dispersion of souls from our midst and our spiritual incapacity. Why? Because we are so flooded with love messages that holy grief gives way to a simple, 'I'm sorry' but we easily fall back to the same old errors. We are so filled with complacency that we do not hunger and thirst, but rather try to find excuses, push blame away from ourselves and even twist Scripture to suit our purpose or even manufacture plausible excuses to explain why prayers are not answered.

Where is the grief? Where is the personal responsibility? Where is the willingness to ask, 'where am I getting this wrong?' What must I do to get on track?

When we sin and disobey God's Word please let's not play with words to make ourselves feel better, the plain fact is we are directly sinning against God Himself. It is not just a wrongdoing in our life; it is a wrongdoing directly against God. It is as if you are throwing dirt in His face!

When we do not respond as Nehemiah did in holy grief, anguish and sorrow; confessing our failings with tears we fall short of walking the Christian life as it should really be lived. We fall short of receiving the power and riches of Heaven and our temple becomes a ruined shadow of its true glory and potential. Let's therefore decide today to stop the rot and decay of our temple and re-build it by seeking the Kingdom with all our heart so that Jesus will not turn to us and say, *'I never knew you; depart from me, you evil doers.'* (Matthew 7: 23)

'Ah but', some might say. Do you know there is always someone somewhere who will come up with a 'but' or a seeming need to voice their opinion instead of looking at the overall picture and going to God first? Having said this there are also the genuine heart questions born from a real longing to know and understand Scripture and follow its ways. It is this attitude to God and His Word that I thoroughly condone. With an attitude of openness to the Holy Spirit let's look at a question that arises from Matthew 7: 13 – 23. It is in this Scripture where we read that there will be many that come to the Lord. Many will prophesy, cast out demons and even do some incredible works but Jesus will say, *'I never knew you; depart from me, you evildoers'* (v23). The heartfelt question that this poses is, 'has this Scripture sent us a 'curved ball' regarding our salvation'?

The Heart of Salvation

I have called this a 'curved ball' because it begs the question, how can we reconcile what Jesus said in Matthew 7: 23, *'I never knew you; depart from me'* with what Paul said to the house churches in Rome, *'For whosoever shall call upon the name of the Lord shall be saved'* (Romans 10: 13).

Perhaps at first glance it would certainly seem that we have uncovered a conflict between what Paul wrote to the house churches and what Jesus Himself actually said. Did Paul make a mistake? Well first, let me say Paul did not make a mistake and actually there is no conflict between what Paul said and the uncompromising statement of Jesus. Secondly, there are some very important issues arising from this question.

Reconciling these seemingly conflicting statements of Matthew chapter seven and Romans chapter ten raises a very important point about the danger of both taking Scripture out of context and only highlighting a sample of a verse, thereby making it read whatever we might wish it to say. This is something that is typically done by those who want to make their own personal point instead of earnestly seeking what God is actually saying.

The setting in which Jesus was speaking is tightly wrapped in what we call the Sermon on the Mount, which covers a range of points talking about living a life of faith and discipleship. The context of the Scripture highlighted in Matthew chapter seven comes at the end of the recorded sermons and follows Jesus' message to take the narrow road that leads to Heaven, watching out for false teachers and warning that it is not enough to simply talk about and outwardly act as if we are disciples but that we must genuinely own our faith and discipleship.

In this scenario of what we might term today as talking the walk versus walking the talk Jesus said, *'Not everyone who says to me, 'Lord, Lord,' shall enter the kingdom of heaven, but he who does the will of my Father who is in heaven'* (Matthew 7: 21). In other words, the guidelines were clearly stated, it is not enough to talk the walk; there is a qualifying clause that we have to do the will of God. With this said, Jesus then explained that on the day of judgement, *'many will say to me, 'Lord, Lord, did we not prophesy in your name, and cast out demons in your name, and do many mighty works in your name?' And then will I declare o them, 'I never knew you; depart from me, you evildoers.'* (Matthew 7: 22, 23)[6]

Can you see that these people knew what words to use and how to act as if they were disciples but they did not actually know Jesus, and He did not know them in relational terms?

When we turn to view what Paul was saying to the Roman Church we discover that he was not, as some surmise, saying all we need to do is call on the name of the Lord and our salvation is definitely secured. We have already discovered that simply calling on the name of Jesus is not enough so let's take a closer look at what Paul was actually saying.

The first thing to appreciate is that the words of Romans 10: 13, which say *'For, 'every one who calls upon the name of the Lord will be saved'* come as a brief summary statement resulting from the key discussions of the previous verses. To simply take this verse out of its context and the rest of Scripture may satisfy some but, as I have already said, I do not want to mis-sell the requirements and consequences of the Christian walk.

When we look at verse nine of Romans chapter ten we discover it says, *'if you confess with your lips that Jesus is Lord and believe in your heart that God raised him from the dead, you will be saved'* (Romans 10: 9). The next verse presses the point home and says, *'For man believes with his heart and so is justified, and he confesses with his lips and so is saved'* (Romans 10: 10). It is the heart where what we

---

6   It may help many reading these words to also look at Luke 8: 5 – 15 (The parable of the sower). It is quite clear here that there are four types of people who hear God's Word, the gospel message (seed). Those likened to:
1.   The path immediately reject the gospel message because satan snatches it from them.
2.   The rock receive the gospel message but then succumb to temptations and slip away.
3.   The thorn receive the gospel message but the pleasures and cares of worldly living pull them away.
4.   The good soil faithfully cling on to what they have received and bear fruit.

truly believe resides and what is in our heart is what we speak and what we speak is how we act and behave.

Head knowledge, or simply saying something, is not enough. It is a matter of what our heart believes and declares. It is what comes from our soul or spirit. In other words what is in our heart, the core of our soul and spirit is what matters.

Chapter ten of the New Testament book of Romans is only part of the discussion that starts in chapter one and continues throughout the entire book. In fact Paul explains why he writes these words both in chapter fifteen and when he outlined the theme of his letter in chapter 1: 16, 17 where he states, *'He who through faith is righteous.'*

When Scripture talks about believing in our heart, it is referring to what lies deep in our soul and spirit. It is about what we truly believe and act upon. That is why we read in Mark 11: 20 - 25 the key to the power of faith is that we do not doubt in our heart. It is the heart where a total and unwavering trust, commitment and belief stem from. It is immoveable and unshakeable and requires action. And Paul actually acknowledges in chapter 14: 23 that whatever does not come from the foundation (or heart) of faith is sin.

As I have said, it is what we believe in our heart that causes us to act and behave in certain ways. The deeper our heart belief, the more tenacious we become in our reflection of what lies in our heart. This point is powerfully expressed in Matthew 15: 18 where we read, *'what comes out of the mouth proceeds from the heart'* and again we read in Luke 6: 45, *'The good man out of the good treasure of his heart produces good, and the evil man out of his evil treasure produces evil.'*

With all of this said there is a salutary twist that should keep us all alert because Scripture warns us time and again to protect our heart, saying *'keep your heart with all vigilance'* (Proverbs 4: 23) and so we are also warned, *'Be sober, be watchful. Your adversary the devil prowls around like a roaring lion, seeking some one to devour'* (1 Peter 5: 8). If we needed to highlight this Scripture verse it actually becomes clearer when we look at the Greek word for devour, which is **katapino** and means to swallow or destroy. In other words, we can easily be swallowed-up and destroyed by the devil. We are all prone to being devoured by our arch-enemy and it is via our hearts that we are vulnerable:

- Hebrews 3: 8 - we can harden our hearts
- Hebrews 3: 10 - we can go astray in our hearts
- Acts 28: 27 - we can grow dull in our hearts
- Acts 8: 21 - our hearts can fail to be right with God
- Mark 7: 6 - our hearts can be far from God

The message that I would like to emphasize is, don't take any risks working out your salvation - keep going to the end. It is worth every one of us heeding the warnings of Scripture. So, let's remind ourselves of just a few to think about with the help of the Holy Spirit and pray over:

- *"No one who puts his hand to the plough and looks back is fit for the Kingdom"* (Luke 9: 62).
- The parable of the sower Mark 4: 3 - 9 - clearly tells us that some initially took the word and believed but failed to continue.
- Some who first believed will become antichrists 1 John 2: 19
- Writing to Timothy Paul said, *'I have fought the good fight, I have finished the race, I have kept the faith. Henceforth there is laid up for me the crown of righteousness'* (2 Timothy 4: 6 - 8).
- *'The gate is narrow and the way is hard, that leads to life, and those who find it are few'* (Matthew 7: 14).

Let no one be mistaken, both the stakes and the costs are high. The greatest potential tragedy facing many in the church today is when the trumpet sound heralding the return of Jesus blasts and He comes, only to leave unprepared people in the church behind.

'I appeal to you therefore, brethren, by the mercies of God, to present your bodies as a living sacrifice, holy and acceptable to God, which is your spiritual worship. Do not be conformed to this world but be transformed by the renewal of your mind, that you may prove what is the will of God, what is good and acceptable and perfect.' (Romans 12: 1, 2)

Food for Thought:

'I preached to you the gospel, which you received, in which you stand, by which you are saved, if you hold it fast – unless you believed in vain.' (1 Corinthians 15: 1, 2)

Chapter Two

Transformation and Renewal

'Do not be conformed to this world but be transformed by the renewal of your mind, that you may prove what is the will of God, what is good and acceptable and perfect.' (Romans 12: 2)

Introduction

Although the First World War is sometimes called 'The Great War', in reality there was little or nothing great about it at all.

As we look back one hundred years it is difficult for us to get inside the mind and mentality of leaders who watched from a distance as they ordered wave after wave of ill-prepared soldiers, to emerge from the relative safety of their trenches to face the unprotected field of bullets, barbed –wire, mud and massacre.

It seems that these well-educated leaders had fixed their minds on one form of warfare, and were unmoved in their thinking by the scale of slaughter they saw to consider what they were doing was not working.

In truth, some of these army officers could see the futility of what was happening, but did not want to question those ranked above them whilst others blindly carried on with thoughts of an honourable and brave death.

This was a war where previously learned tactics were outdated by superior 'modern' machinery and fire-power and so I am not trying to use clever hindsight to accuse the leaders of being incompetent fools, but it does paint a picture of failure to learn from mistakes and realize that when something does not work it is highly likely to continue not to work.

I wonder how many countless lives could have been saved if bold and thoughtful action had been positively taken sooner? How many soldiers would have avoided the pointless massacre if leaders had not conformed to the mind-numbing traditions and stopped the slaughter of man against bullet by taking time to think about a new approach much sooner?

We might innocently look at the exhibited foolishness of the First World War and think we would not make the same mistakes. Yet in our Christian spiritual war against a well-equipped and cunning foe, is it not the case that we, all too often ill-prepared, engage in a war of attrition and massacre in a similar mindless way?

How many of us look at the spiritual battlefield and its carnage in our churches and the death of souls in society but fail to consider that what we are doing is not working effectively? How many leaders and pastors can see what is happening but are too afraid to say and do something? How many leaders look at the awful destruction and effectively say that it was a noble defeat and death?

Why do so many in the church silently say, 'I know things are not right' and yet do nothing and carry on as they are? Worse still, are churches that talk about the problems but do not plan for or expect to see change. Surely it is time to realize that if what we are doing is inadequate and does not work it is time to think again, change direction and obey God's word?

The problem for the church is that we have locked ourselves into centuries of man-inspired entrenched ways of thinking and our minds have become clouded by our experiences, our limitations and our efforts to find solutions.

Too many spiritual lives have been lost and too much damage has been caused because we have been guilty of engaging in man's tactics, understanding and ways. It is time to put behind us the habits and wisdom of man. What we need is a complete mind overhaul so that we live and act totally immersed in God's ways and are equipped with His fire-power; a power that has lain untapped and dormant in the majority of us.

Surely enough is enough? Surely now is the time and opportunity to break the ties and cut ourselves loose from the destructive conformity of a man-centred worldly based church thinking and focus our attention on what God says.

The Conformed Mind

In chapter twelve of his letter to the Roman churches Paul urged them not to conform to the world. Our understanding of conformity to the world today probably means to not act and behave like the rest of the world, and sure enough that is part of what Paul was saying. But if we look at the original Greek word for *conform* in Romans 12: 2 we find the translated word **systchematizo**, which reveals a much deeper and fundamental meaning because it speaks not simply about our outwardly seen behaviour, (which can easily be switched on and off according to the situation and environment we find ourselves in) but about the conformity of our mind and the person we really are; our character.

The point I am making is one we are all aware of because there are many Christian believers who act one way in church environments but quite differently away from it. For others, there are old worldly habits and behaviours that remain unchanged in their lives and so there is a sort of dual-personality that is neither fully in one camp nor the other. This happens because many believers have come to Christ but have not dealt with or changed their mindset. They are still conformed to their former worldly life because their mind remains unchanged and fundamentally unaffected.

An unchanged mind will always produce an unchanged character because what the mind is freely allowed to feed upon, through the data input channels of our eyes and ears, is what we think about. What we think about is what we conform ourselves to. What we conform to is how we behave and how we behave is who we are; our character. It is for this reason that Proverbs says, *'the mind of a man reflects the man.'* (Proverbs 27: 19)

Dealing with the problem of an unchanged mind in his first letter Peter writes:

'gird up your minds, be sober, set your hope fully upon the grace that is coming to you at the revelation of Jesus Christ. As obedient children, do not be conformed to the passions of your former ignorance, but as he who called you is holy, be holy yourselves in all your conduct; since it is written, 'You shall be holy, for I am holy.' (1 Peter 1: 13 – 16)

Peter opens this Scripture with the words, **'gird up your minds.'** This may seem to us reading it today a very strange thing to say, but for the Greco-Roman audience girding-up was something quite normal to them. Girding-up an item of clothing was a common practice because it allowed greater freedom of movement. For example, gathering-up or girding-up a long robe to run gave freedom for the legs to stretch out unhindered by the close-fitting long garment. The power of the mind was also something that was not lost on the listening audience. In relating the idea of girding-up the mind, what Peter was saying is we must gather-up the constraints of our old ways of thinking by binding our mind or what he called being, *'conformed to the passions of your former ignorance'* (v14) so that we give it freedom to take a different and godly perspective. Paul referred to this similar process as taking, *'every thought captive.'* (2 Corinthians 10: 5)

It is an amazing experience to take our thoughts and make them captive to Jesus. As soon as anything we wish to remove from our thinking is taken to Jesus our obedience is rewarded with clarity and holy peace.

What Peter and Paul were explaining, is that the mind is where our thoughts, convictions, bias and beliefs conform to what we allow it to engage with through our eyes, ears and feelings as well as the influences of our up-bringing, teaching and the people we mix with. We are influenced by the worldly attractions, philosophies and influences that we have grown up with. Much of this feeds our ego and naturally sinful make-up. But we are now followers of Jesus and so Paul eloquently and pertinently explains:

'If then you have been raised with Christ, seek the things that are above, where Christ is, seated at the right hand of God. Set your minds on things that are above, not on things that are on earth. For you have died, and your life is hid with Christ in God. When Christ who is our life appears, then you also will appear with him in glory.' (Colossians 3: 1 – 4)

Breaking the strangle-hold of a conformed mind means that we must firmly set our minds on Heavenly things or as Paul explained in Romans chapter 12, we must transform our thinking.

The Renewed Mind

It is the renewal of our mind that brings transformation in our spiritual lives. Or put another way, we cannot transform our spiritual thinking if we do not renew it. This renewal takes a deliberate and conscious action on our part. It is a voluntary act of permanently turning or repenting from a worldly-centred and focused mind to a Heavenly-centred and focused mind.

The turning of the focus of our mind is crucial to a holy life and so talking about the dangers of friendship with the world James makes a startling and uncompromising statement highlighting the fact that *'friendship with the world is enmity with God'* (James 4: 4). Gosh, what a powerful statement of fact. James plainly tells us that if we do not deal with our worldly focused minds we are at enmity with God! I am not sure how much clearer Scripture can really be but if that does not shake us to our senses Paul is even more straightforward and makes this stunning declaration to the members of the Roman church:

'For those who live according to the flesh set their minds on the things of the flesh, but those that live according to the Spirit set their minds on the things of the Spirit. To set the mind on the flesh is death, but to set the mind on the Spirit is life and peace. For the mind that is set on the flesh is hostile to God; it does not submit to God's law, indeed it cannot; and those who are in the flesh cannot please God.' (Romans 8: 5 – 8)

Yes, this is a message to the church! It is a message to you and me. It is not a declaration that any Christian believer can simply shrug-off, make light of or turn-around and point at unbelievers.

The enmity and hostility of an unchanged mind toward God is a truth that needs to be brought to the forefront of our minds; a truth that we must not let out of our sight. It is a truth telling us clearly that it is not enough to simply speak words of belief in Jesus or even do and say the right things, we must take positive action, renew our mind and yield ourselves totally to God (James 4: 7).

This is a message so powerfully important that it is worth stressing the point being made by James and Paul, which is our minds are either at enmity with God or in harmony with Him. There is no mid-way; it is one or the other. We either think like Him or we think our own opposing thoughts. The stark outcome is that anyone who is at enmity with God will not enter the Kingdom of Heaven and into God's holy realm.

Now in making these comments I am aware that some readers may become agitated, dislike the words and go on the offensive. Others will read the follow-on verses of Romans 8: 9 – 11, which provide a 'but' and speak of being in the Spirit and alive. Reading this, they do not look at the context and may even turn the Scripture to point at others, thinking they themselves are safe and having done this, negate the words of Scripture by immediately forgetting the crucial importance of renewing their own mind. This common process is a terrible and costly pit to fall into. You see Paul qualified his comments by saying, *'if in fact the Spirit of God dwells in you'* (Romans 8: 9). Here Paul uses that key word 'if' and in doing so points back to what he had already said in verse five, *'those that live according to the Spirit set their minds on the things of the*

Spirit' (Romans 8: 5). In other words, a renewed mind is one that lives according to the Spirit. It cannot help its focus and commitment to the things of the Spirit. It rejects the worldly or fleshly desires and both looks heavenward and like Jesus lives Heaven on earth. Or put another way, it is through the renewed mind that we bring the supernatural life of Heaven to earth. The key here is then a renewed mind. Great, but how do we renew our mind?

Renewing the Mind

The reason our minds need renewing is because up and until we gave our lives to Christ, our experience of life, our involvement in it and our knowledge and thinking were constantly filled with worldly, sinful, egoistic and man inspired influences which have taken root within us. The Kingdom of Heaven is completely opposite to our upbringing. It is not worldly, it is Heavenly. It is not sinful; it is sinless, pure and holy. It is not egoistic; it is selfless, submissive and loving. It is not man inspired and faithless; it is God-inspired and faithful. Put simply, if our mind is not renewed and made receptive to the Kingdom of Heaven's way of thinking, our lives will not transform.

To answer the question 'how do we renew our mind' we have to take an important and personally costly first step. At this point I have to warn you, it is a step from which we can never return or look back. Having said this, it is equally true that if we are unwilling to take this step we will not progress in our Christian lives. This fact was dramatically made clear to me some years ago as I was out walking and talking with the Lord.

I had reached a stage where I knew my Christian life was not what it should really be. It looked okay from the outside but in my spirit I knew there was more and, if honest the real power of God was missing. Please do not misunderstand, I was baptized in the Holy Spirit with speaking in tongues and I had witnessed people being healed when I prayed for them. I had laid hands over people and even without touching them, had seen some falling under the power of the Spirit, and I had given prophecies that came to fruition but I knew there was more available to me. Something was not quite right; something was causing me to miss the fullness that I read in Scripture but somehow and somewhere I was aware that a blockage was preventing the flow and I needed to know why.

The only way I can think to describe my Christian walk was a bit like a blocked water drainpipe. The water was flowing into the drain but little of it was passing through to other pipes taking it to a collection pool. Most of it was flowing back out of the drain from where it had entered. It had become ineffective and worse still, causing damage to the surrounding areas of my life a bit like stagnant water damages the ground upon which it sits. Something in the pipe was obviously blocking the natural flow. It was not until I determined to push the drain rods of total surrender through the pipework that I removed the blockage and the water flowed freely.

What we must fully understand is that it is not Scripture or God that is the blockage; it is to us - you and me. If we do not reach this point of honest realization, and hunger and thirst we will not decide in our hearts to use the 'clearing rods.' We will not clear the blockages that we have created. You see, a blocked drain becomes blocked because something has become lodged in it; a foreign object that has no rightful place there. As these foreign objects mount so the blockage builds to a point where they can only be unblocked by forceful action. That is why we read about men who take the Kingdom of Heaven by force (Matthew 11: 12). There are times when we are going to have to take drastic action and fight like combat soldiers for the Kingdom. This, for all of us, is one of those times!

Knowing that I had to do something about my walk with God, I began not only just to call out but literally shout at the top of my voice to God asking Him what I needed to do. I have to tell you, God remained totally silent and seemingly unaffected by my shouts and tears. I began to say, 'surely what I was asking; to go deeper with the Lord is a good thing.' The continued silence made me shout more and with a spiritual anger I blurted out, 'Lord God don't you care?' All I was asking for was more of God; surely this could not be wrong? Yet still more silence followed. I reached an agonizing cross-road; give up or push on.

Standing at the cross-road, even the increased intensity of my shouts were simply followed by more silence, a silence so powerful in its effect that it eventually made me say something like, 'okay Lord, I give in. I give you my heart, mind, soul, spirit and body.' It was all I could think of in my desperation; a heartfelt desperation that then said, 'I will go where you want me to go.' I immediately felt a little calmer, almost as if these were words that I had not spoken out before but they needed confessing and vocalizing audibly. I suppose it was an open admission of my deeper feelings and shortcomings.

What happened next was both a complete shock and totally unexpected. God finally spoke and He asked a question in the form of these three powerful words, 'whatever it takes?' There was no price tag attached to the question. No clues about the future, and absolutely no promises or assurances.

Here I was; I had just offered God everything and He asked for more! I was, if you prefer, offered a take it or leave it challenge. It was a question of asking for the entire package or nothing.

This all or nothing commitment is what Jesus meant when He said, *'If any man will come after me, let him deny himself and take up his cross daily and follow me. For whoever would save his life will lose it; and whoever loses his life for my sake, he will save it'* (Luke 9: 23, 24). These words of Jesus are familiar to most of us but their impact is rarely taught with the passion and honesty that Jesus meant them. Let's be absolutely clear, there is no fence-sitting. We cannot give part of ourselves to the Christian walk. The cross we take up when we come to Jesus is not a once-off action. The cross we take up is a cross that must be taken up every day of our lives.

The problem for many of us is that we have wrongly been sold a sugar-coated Christianity of promises and security that are simply so far from the truth that it is going to leave some not only disappointed but outside of the Kingdom of Heaven. The sweet-smelling promises that all you need to do is say a prayer, go to church, do a few good things, believe in Jesus and all is well because God loves you is nothing more than a grand deception. Yes, of course these are precious truths in their right context but they are cleverly wrapped up in this deception. But that is what makes it so attractive and compelling. Like all good lies and deceptions the closer it is to the truth the more effective the sting.

The stark reality of the Christian life is that it is a life of repentance, love, forgiveness and total commitment to the Lord. It is a life that has died to self-desire and passions and lives instead in harmony with Christ. It is a life of holiness, godly love and supernatural power. It is a life proactively determined to do the will of God and that which is pleasing to Him.

But of course all of this now begs the question what is:
1. The will of God?
2. What pleases God?

The Will of God

The will of God is clearly explained in Paul's first letter to the church of Thessalonica where he says, *'For this is the will of God, your sanctification'* (1 Thessalonians 4: 3).

The Greek word used here for sanctification is **hagiasmos** meaning being purified and holy. When we come to Christ it is the beginning of the journey of sanctification, which is only made possible by the covering of His sacrificed body and blood. Separating ourselves from sin begins when we give our lives to Jesus. But, to stop at this point, as many have unfortunately been misled to believe and simply rest in what Jesus did on the cross is not enough. It will not on its own get us through the narrow gate to Heaven, because we have to do our part or we may actually be in danger of falling away. That is why God wants us to keep growing in sanctification, so that none of us fall short.

Now it is at this point that the mis-selling of the Christian faith kicks-in because many will say, 'I prayed the prayer of salvation and so I am heaven-bound.' But no consideration is given to the Scriptures already highlighted in this chapter. Almost, it seems conveniently Scriptures such as, *'Not every one who says to me, 'Lord, Lord,' shall enter the kingdom of heaven, but he who does the will of my Father who is in heaven'* (Matthew 7: 21) are quietly pushed behind the scenes and no heed is then paid to the words of Jesus who said, *'many will fall away'* (Matthew 24: 10).

What did Jesus mean when He said, *'fall away'*? The Greek word used here is **skandalizo**, which means to induce sinfulness, displease, offend or desert. Peter warned that there will be false teachers arising from among our own ranks in the church, those whom beforehand had been followers bringing in destructive heresies (2 Peter 2: 1)[7]. And the writer of Hebrews tells us, *'it is impossible to restore again to repentance those who have once been enlightened, who have tasted the heavenly gift, and have become partakers of the Holy Spirit'* (Hebrews 6: 4). How much clearer can the warnings be? It seems to me that we take a huge risk with our salvation if we do not strive toward holiness. We can argue the Scriptures but is the risk worth it? And in any case, why would any of us want less than holiness?

The point is Jesus has done His part in planting the seed of sanctification in us when we come to Him and we have, from that time forward, to do our part to nurture this seed to maturity and become what Jesus has started in us.

Sanctification is all about the person we are; our true character. It is a life-long process of dying more and more to self and sin and growing more and more in holiness. Paul put it this way, *'consider yourselves dead to sin and alive to God in Christ Jesus'* (Romans 6: 11). It is a process that we undertake throughout our entire life. We cannot be in the same place yesterday as we are today; we must constantly be moving forward.

What pleases God?

There are two key areas of our lives that please God. The first really follows the theme of what I have already been talking about and is found in Psalm 19: 14, *'Let the words of my mouth*

---

7   2 Peter 2: 1 – *'But false prophets also arose among the people, just as there will be false teachers among you, who will secretly bring in destructive heresies, even denying the Master who brought them, bringing upon themselves swift destruction.'*

and the meditation of my heart Be acceptable in Your sight, O Lord, my strength and my redeemer' (NKJV). It is all about what we put into our minds, think constantly about and the truths that lie in the depth of our heart that make us who we are. Here the Psalmist, in an act of humble commitment seeks to confirm that everything in his life is acceptable and pleasing to God.

Linked closely to what we should focus our minds upon the writer to the Hebrews simply says, *'And without faith it is impossible to please him'* (Hebrews 11: 6). In other words, if we do not come to that point of faith where we give all our trust and confidence to God in the assurance that He will do what He says, we fail to act in a way pleasing to Him.

Now logically if as it says in Leviticus 11: 44 and 1 Peter 1: 16 it is the will of God that we become holy as He is holy, and it pleases Him when our speech and meditation not only focus on Him but cause us to become like Him in our faith; a faith that not only knows that it knows, but lives in the realm of possibilities and miracles. Isn't it strange that these things are the exception and not the norm in daily Christian lives and the life of the church?

Something clearly is not quite right and needs re-adjusting in our thinking or as Paul said to the Roman churches, *'be transformed by the renewal of your mind, that you may prove what is the will of God, what is good and acceptable and perfect'* (Romans 12: 2). Here, through Paul's words it is obvious that if we want to transform our lives we have to deal with our minds and renew our thinking.

Understanding the Mind

This may come as a surprise to some, but renewing the mind is not something that just happens automatically when we become Christians. If it were there would be no need for phrases speaking to the Christian believer such as the *'mind set on the flesh'* (Romans 8: 7) or *'do not be conformed to this world'* (Romans 12: 2). These Scripture verses, along with other similar ones are there because naturally our mind, which is sinfully connected, remains in its former sinful state when we first come to the Lord. What I am saying is that the mind needs revamping. In this sense it is, for the majority of us, a second stage process in our overall salvation journey; one that today we would generally understand and describe as moving from head (mind) knowledge to heart knowledge. Or put another way, it's the difference between knowing the theory and knowing the practical and revelatory experience. It is the stage that moves us from worldly living to spiritual living.

What I've described here is a mind that is not only at odds with God but it seems to have different functioning levels, which I have already simply called, head and heart knowledge. Interestingly, man in his own wisdom has come to understand how the mind works through the study of psychology and there are parallels with what we read about the mind in Scripture, which are worth investigating so that we can gain a better grasp of what the Bible is telling us. So let's briefly scrutinize the psychology based on how the mind operates because it is here where we find three helpful basic levels of the mind's function known as the conscious, preconscious and unconscious mind that expose some interesting things that we might now recognize in Scripture and ourselves.

The conscious mind is where information through the eyes, ears and senses is initially received by each of us. Once received the mind familiarizes the information and thoughts by mentally processing and rationalizing them in harmony with the preconscious mind where previously stored knowledge and experiences are held. The unconscious mind is where what we have thought about, rationalized and processed, mix with the memory of known positive or negative experiences. These conclusions are then stored as our beliefs in the unconscious mind.

The unconscious mind does not have a right and wrong filter. It simply accepts the end product of our thoughts and experiences as beliefs. The actions, speech and behaviours we then display in our daily lives imitate our beliefs. For example, if at the conscious level, a person receives information that repeatedly tells them they are a failure and they try something a few times and do not succeed this information will process in the conscious mind as, 'I was previously told I am a failure.' The preconscious mind then says,

'I was told I am a failure, I have failed and so I must actually be a failure.' The person will now hold the belief that they are a failure in their unconscious mind and so they act according to their belief as a failure even though it is not true.

Making changes to this pattern of thinking and beliefs is what being transformed by the renewal of our minds is all about. It is about breaking the false and sinful pattern that we have allowed to enter our minds. It is about breaking connection with the influences of the negative sinful world and willfully submitting ourselves to God and the Holy Spirit so that we follow holy patterns and truths.

Of course the Bible does not use the same twentieth century technical terms used by modern-day psychology but it does speak about the mind in three ways. So let's first take a look at what the Old Testament has to say.

The ancient Hebrew word for mind is **leb** (or also written **lebab**), which has two roots because the heart and soul, which I will explain in more detail shortly, are interchangeably used in Scripture and closely tied together:

- The first part of **leb** or **lebab** is where information enters the mind and understanding; knowledge, thinking and solutions take place. This is what psychology calls the mind or conscious mind. So as an example, in Proverbs 16: 9 we read – *'A man's mind* (leb) *plans his way, but the Lord directs his steps.'*

- The second part of **leb** or **lebab** joins the heart and soul together and refers to the part of the mind where self-will, man's wisdom and moral character and beliefs take place. In psychology this is the preconscious and unconscious mind). For example, Proverbs 27: 19 – *'As in water face answers to face, so the mind* (leb sometimes translated as heart) *of a man reflects the man.'*

These same aspects of the mind are found again in the New Testament where Jesus, for example acknowledges three different levels of the mind and He repeats Deuteronomy 6: 5 in these words,

'You shall love the Lord your God with all your heart, and with all your soul, and with all your mind' (Matthew 22: 37). When we look closely at the Greek words for heart, soul and mind used by Jesus in this statement we find:

- Heart – The Greek word **kardia** meaning the soul or mind, the centre or seat of spiritual life and purpose. As we probe a little deeper we discover two very different conditions of a man's heart. The heart that is worldly and sinful harbours such things as hatred as described by the attitude of Michal the daughter of Saul who saw King David leaping and dancing before the Lord, *'and she despised him in her heart'* (2 Samuel 6: 16). Or pride as mentioned in Proverbs 21: 4, which says, *'Haughty eyes and a proud heart, the lamp of the wicked, are sin.'* The Psalmist however reminds us that, *'He who has clean hands and a pure heart, who does not lift up his soul to what is false, and does not swear deceitfully'* (Psalm 24: 4) is a person with a heart that has turned to God and been made pure. Mark also talks about the effect of a God centred heart in a person who *'does not doubt in his heart.'* (Mark 11: 23)

- Soul – The Greek word here is **psyche** meaning soul or spirit, the seat of the mind's spiritual nature, feelings, affections, life and desires. Again there are two opposing states of the soul and so we read, *'The soul of the wicked desires evil'* (Proverbs 21: 10) or *'the soul that sins shall die'* (Ezekiel 18: 4). Alternatively Peter says, *'Having purified your souls by your obedience to the truth for a sincere love of the brethren, love one another earnestly from the heart.'* (1 Peter 1: 22)

- Mind – From the Greek word **dianoia** for thoughts, thinking, reasoning and understanding. Again, as we have already discovered the thoughts and thinking of a person are either *'conformed to this world'* (Romans 12: 2) and at enmity with God (Romans 8: 7) or renewed so that we *'may prove what is the will of God, what is good and acceptable and perfect.'* (Romans 12: 2)

So in Scripture we can clearly see how the pattern and sources of information entering the mind are easily assimilated and pass through our moral and spiritual filter before being accepted as a belief. What we believe becomes how we behave and how we behave is the person or character that we are. The end product depends on whether the mind is worldly conformed or spiritually transformed. Scripture has shown us that the mind is easily influenced by what the Bible calls the flesh or Spirit or what psychology calls the personality traits id, super-ego and ego.

Sin Personified

The sinful nature of man and particularly that of a Christian is something that rarely, if ever, receives the attention it should in our churches today.

Understanding the id, super-ego and ego personality traits will help us to unravel some deeper biblical truths about the Christian believer's sinful condition. It will sharpen our attention toward God and help us increase our determination to take positive and urgent action:

- The id refers to the basic, uncoordinated and impulsive instincts that infiltrate the mind. It is not based on logic or reality but characterized by its impulsive pleasure-seeking and craving for immediate satisfaction. The Bible calls id the flesh and says, *'do not gratify the desires of the flesh. For the desires of the flesh are against the Spirit'* (Galatians 5: 16, 17). And again, *'the mind that is set on the flesh is hostile to God'* (Romans 8: 7). What we can see from this is that the id or flesh connects directly to our sinful nature and is an open entry point that satan uses unless we refuse to gratify these desires and close the door to him. If we do not deal with our conformity to the world we are at enmity with God.

- The super-ego indicates our moral standard that balances the instincts of the id and can suppress unacceptable behaviour by stopping us from doing what the id would otherwise want us to do. But there is a danger here that we must fully understand because the super-ego is either worldly or heavenly influenced. The worldly influenced standard is clearly articulated in Proverbs as, *'All the ways of a man are pure in his own eyes, but the Lord weighs the spirit'* (Proverbs 16: 2). And, *'Every way of a man is right in his own eyes, but the Lord weighs the heart'* (Proverbs 21: 2). The Lord weighs the source of our actions. Conformity to the world leads to worldly moral standards. Renewal in the Spirit leads to heavenly standards.

- The ego has many of the characteristics of the id, but they are also influenced and modified by its experience of the world so that it can find ways of realistically and socially satisfying the id's demands. In Scripture the ego is *'conformed to this world'* (Romans 12: 2), and again, *'conformed to the passions of your former ignorance'* (1 Peter 1: 14). We can combat this by humbling ourselves and so that is why Peter says, *'Humble yourselves therefore under the mighty hand of God, that in due time he may exalt you.'*

Most of us would recognize the id and super-ego as the voice (id) speaking in one ear goading us to do something whilst in the other ear the voice (super-ego) is applying either a worldly or godly moral standard.

- It is through the id and ego that satan operates. They are naturally impulsive-pleasure seeking parts of our sinful nature that either act uncontrollably (id) or act in a way consistent with worldly standards (ego). This is why the Bible speaks of such things as:
- *'Out of the heart come evil thoughts'* (Matthew 15: 19)
- *'I was brought forth in iniquity, and in sin did my mother conceive me'* (Psalm 51: 5)
- *'The wicked go astray from the womb, they err from their birth, speaking lies'* (Psalm 58: 3)

But why is all of this so important? Well the first thing for us to realize is that transformation can only take place in the id, super-ego and ego when we wilfully hand these parts of ourselves to God and then work hard to uphold thoughts consistent with His. James summarizes much of what I have said in these words, *'God opposes the proud, but gives grace to the humble.' Submit yourselves therefore to God. Resist the devil and he will flee from you. Draw near to God and he will draw near to you. Cleanse your hands, you sinners, and purify your hearts, you men of double mind.'* (James 4: 6 – 8)

None of us should become lulled into any form of misunderstanding or complacency. James is addressing Christian believers; that is you and me. James makes no apology for his straight talking and we should seek no self-defense. We are believers *'of double mind'* (James 4: 8) when we conform to the world. And, *'a double-minded man, unstable in all his ways'* (James 1: 7, 8), will receive nothing from God.

Double Mind

We cannot attach ourselves to two different beliefs and standards at the same time. Scripture makes it clear to us that we cannot be connected to worldly beliefs and at the same time the beliefs and standards of the Spirit of God. *'For those who live according to the flesh set their minds on the things of the flesh, but those that live according to the Spirit set their minds on the things of the Spirit'* (Romans 8: 5). In psychological terms where two contradictory beliefs converge it is known as cognitive dissonance. This theory agrees with Scripture that two beliefs cannot co-exist so what happens is the unconscious mind makes adjustments or a best-fit.

What I have described as the best-fit is where Christian believers who are still conformed to the world live their lives. This is because all the time any of us stay conformed to the world we create a blockage to the deeper, supernatural things of God and we cannot move entirely into and fully understand the things of God. We have to 'best-fit' the Bible around the dominant constraints of worldly thinking.

It is like trying to serve two masters at the same time. Jesus explained that, *'No servant can serve two masters; for either he will hate the one and love the other, or he will be devoted to the one, and despise the other'* (Luke 16: 13). This scenario is really part of what Paul prophesied to Timothy about people in the church when he said, *'For the time is coming when people will not endure sound teaching, but having itching ears they will accumulate for themselves teachers to suit their own likings, and will turn away from listening to the truth and wander into myths'* (2 Timothy 4: 3, 4). When we conform ourselves to the world we seek out those things that will satisfy our likings and beliefs.

The tragedy of what I am talking about is that many believers think they are perfectly okay; after all they became a Christian! But actually they do not have a revelatory understanding of God. Jeremiah helps us to understand what is happening in this scenario when he said, *'The heart is deceitful above all things, and desperately corrupt* (some Bible versions fittingly say sick)' (Jeremiah 17: 9). What Jeremiah is explaining is that we have a deceitfulness embedded in us, a deceitfulness that blinds us to spiritual truths and which has made us spiritually desperately sick. We, as John also said (1 John 1: 8) *'deceive ourselves'* if we think simply believing in Jesus, saying a prayer, doing some good works or even seeing a few healings means all is well. If this is our conviction then we are as Jeremiah said *'desperately corrupt'* or sick. This is why we have to completely break away from worldly influences and be renewed and transformed.

The point I am stressing is that the transfer of what we have called head to heart knowledge requires our deliberate willingness to yield not only our spiritual body but our mind to God. We need to allow Him to carry out renovations of our mind and renew it by a continuously open conscious and deliberate act of our will. This is why Paul said, *'Put off your old nature which belongs to your former manner of life and is corrupt through deceitful lusts, and be renewed in the spirit of your minds, and put on the new nature, created after the likeness of God in true righteousness and holiness'* (Ephesians 4: 22 – 24). All of this is necessary because a renewed mind is not only totally God friendly, it is the source of our ability to ally ourselves with Heaven and the supernatural lifestyle that we should daily walk in.

The point behind what I am saying will perhaps become clearer if we think about a learning environment. Two people of equal intelligence can hear the same teaching but the outcome is very different. For example teaching on subjects such as revival, the supernatural power of God and healing, produce those that are enthusiastically interested and want it and those that will have no real impact and not want it. The same happens with people who hear the gospel message, some are very interested and others will dismiss it.

Jesus explained what I am saying about hearing the word of God in the parable of the sower found in Luke 8: 4 – 15. All of the people heard what God was saying but for various reasons the response was different:

- Verse 12 – The people heard but, *'the devil comes and takes away the word from their hearts that they may not believe and be saved.'* This is an example of a person who has not just listened but taken what they have heard to their heart. But it is a heart that, as we have already discovered has remained conformed to the world and has not been renewed and turned to God. It has been left open to the devil's attack.

- Verse 13 – This person has joyfully received God's word but they have little or no soil of the Spirit in them for the seed to develop. They are still conformed to the world with an ego that is man-inspired and they are open to the temptations of the devil.

- Verse 14 – There are those so entrenched in the flesh and influence of the id that the word of God is not as important to them as their riches and pleasures.

- Verse 15 – Here we find a person who has renewed their mind and the Spirit has prepared good soil for the seed of God's word to develop. These people have, '***an honest and good heart.***'

What we learn from this is that a mind conformed to the

world can see and hear the things of God but it is not touched and affected by what it sees and hears beyond a superficial level and so it very quickly either switches off or forgets what it has heard. It hears about healings and miracles, it sees them but it cannot go further. This is a mind that thinks what it sees by God's grace is enough and it becomes content and satisfied. But it cannot comprehend the deeper teachings and messages that God is speaking. It cannot grasp the hunger and thirst for more. To the renewed mind it is different, it sees and hears. It sees the possible and the possibilities and is desperately thirsty for more. It reacts in such a positive and eager way that it is open to the Spirit and open to the supernatural lifestyle that should actually be a part of every-day living and experience.

All of this has pointed to a very serious problem in the church. In fact the problem is catastrophic and it partly explains why the church has become supernaturally impotent.

Catastrophe in the Church

What we have learned in this chapter is that the heart (mind) is where man believes (Romans 10: 10). A mind conformed to the world believes in worldly things and worldly ways – it cannot comprehend God's ways of thinking because they are totally opposite, they think differently and act differently.

The mind conformed to the world can only think and see through worldly wisdom. Even though some Bible knowledge and experience exists in a person their conformed mind remains tainted by worldly ways of thinking and imperfections. The conformed mind simply makes adaptations to fit around various aspects of Scripture but it cannot break beyond this or comprehend the things of the Spirit. It cannot grasp the deeper things of God. It is unable to get to grips with the supernatural because it does not have the mind of Christ.

Layer upon layer the church has fallen into a catastrophic state because as a general rule worldly conformed minds are leading those with conformed minds. Conformed minds in the church are teaching conformed understanding of Scripture and creating more conformed minds. What we have created is a vicious circle of conformity with the flesh and sin. We have to break this conformity.

Satan is at work in the church. Jesus explained this in the parable of the wheat and tares found in Matthew 13: 24 - 30. The enemy has planted tares (or weeds) among the wheat. But what are these tares?

The Greek word used for the English translation tares is **zizanion**. Zizanion is a ryegrass that we now call darnel (Latin name lolium temulentum also known as false wheat or weeds), which look exactly like wheat in its early stage of growth and is toxic if eaten.

We shouldn't really be surprised by the fact that toxicity exists in the church but the clear identification of who the true believers are and who are not can often prove extremely difficult to spot, that's why the parable tells us that when asked the owner said no to removing the tares (weeds), *'lest in gathering the weeds you root up the wheat along with them'* (Matthew 13: 29). The truth is, we are vulnerable targets and so we have a personal responsibility to walk in daily obedience to God. It is only when we have truly died to Christ and sacrificed ourselves that we are hid in Him (Colossians 3: 3).

Not one of us, whoever we are or whatever place we might hold in the church will ever move forward from our situation of conformity to the flesh until we obey God and separate from it. The question is, 'have we truly separated ourselves from the flesh?' This is the check that confronts every Christian believer reading these words:

- *'You shall not do as they do in the land of Egypt, where you dwelt, and you shall not do as they do in the land of Canaan, to which I am bringing you. You shall not walk in their statutes'* (Leviticus 18: 3). Are we doing as others are doing in our society and walking in their wisdom?

- *'As obedient children, do not be conformed to the passions of your former ignorance'* (1 Peter 1: 14). Are we obedient and disconnected from our former worldly ignorance?

- *'Do not love the world or the things in the world. If any one loves the world, love for the Father is not in him. For all that is in the world, the lust of the flesh and the lust of the eyes and the pride of life, is not of the Father but is of the world'* (1 John 2: 15, 16). Are we captivated by our love for the world or our love for God?

God has never changed; He has always commanded His people to separate themselves from the world. Paul made this point so strongly to the church in Corinth that it was a command to separate from the world.

What we must understand is that separation from the world is not a suggestion. It is not just a good idea. It is also not an optional extra, it is a command that those who have not separated themselves have disobeyed.

This is the test of our, yours and mine, true commitment to God:

'Do not be mismated with unbelievers. For what partnership have righteousness and iniquity? Or what fellowship has light with darkness? What accord has Christ with Belial? Or what has a believer in common with an unbeliever? What agreement has the temple of God with idols? For we are the temple of the living God.' (2 Corinthians 6: 14 – 16)

No one reading these words can go beyond this point without making a choice. It is a costly decision whichever route any of us might take:

1. Do nothing and continue conformed to this world
2. Take action to commit, renew and be transformed

What happens from this point is of course a personal choice however, before making the choice it might prove worthwhile learning a lesson from the catastrophe the Jewish people of Jerusalem fell into.

The Jewish people of Jeremiah's day had slipped away from God and began to pay attention to other teachings, gods and worldly influences. And so God gave them an opportunity and pleaded, *'O Jerusalem, wash your heart from wickedness, that you may be saved.'* He also asked the people, *'How long shall your evil thoughts lodge within you?"* (Jeremiah 4: 14). God, through Jeremiah, warned the people that they would be judged for their disobedience and maintaining their worldly hearts and ways of thinking. They would be overthrown and lose what they had. Tragically none of this had an effect on the people; they carried on as they were.

These Jewish people could plainly see that things were not right but did nothing about it. They heard the warnings from God but their fleshly conformed minds desensitized them from Him. Yet again God spoke and He said, as He is saying to us today:

'Hear this, O foolish and senseless people; who have eyes, but see not, who have ears, but hear not. Do you not fear me? Says the Lord; Do you not tremble before me?' (Jeremiah 5: 21, 22)

It seems incredible with the benefit of hindsight that the Jewish people could not comprehend what was happening. They did not listen. They thought they were safe and okay, after all, they were God's chosen. Why did they act as they did and ignore God's warnings?

Well we discover the answer in these words:

'But this people has a stubborn and rebellious heart; they have turned aside and gone away. They do not say in their hearts, 'Let us fear the Lord our God, who gives the rain in its season, the autumn rain, and the spring rain, and keeps for us the weeks appointed for the harvest.' (Jeremiah 5: 23)

We can learn from the Jewish people but if none of this stirs something within us and causes us to want to know what we must do something is wrong. Is there a stubborn and rebellious heart in you? Stubbornness and rebellion will, as Jeremiah said, keep eyes blind and ears deaf whilst the humble and contrite will see, hear and act.

What must we do?

James summarized what each Christian believer must do with this simple and precise statement, *'keep oneself unstained from the world'* (James 1: 27).

The renewed mind cannot entertain anything from its past; anything contrary to God's nature. The how is neatly outlined for us by Paul in the third chapter of his letter to the Colossians:

- Verse 2 – *'Set your minds on things that are above, not on things that are on earth.'* There are only two directions in which we can focus our minds; heaven or earth. Our focus must always be heavenward. We must flush our minds with the Holy Spirit, deal with what we allow to enter it through our senses, the eyes and ears and walk in holiness. We must decide in our minds and heart never to resist the Holy Spirit[8] or prevent Him from doing what He wants to do in us. The alternative is a danger we cannot belittle, underestimate or understate. If we take our eyes off God we become stained and ensnared by the world. To those in the church that walk according to the flesh Paul said, *'I warn you as I warned you before, that those that do such things shall not inherit the kingdom of God'* (Galatians 5: 21).

- Verse 5 – *'Put to death therefore what is earthly in you.'* The cost of setting our minds on heaven is our life in exchange for the life of Jesus. It is a deliberate and conscious act of our will. It is, as I mentioned earlier, an all or nothing decision. If we set our will against conforming to our worldly passions, satan cannot stop us. But it must always be a wilful and sustained decision or as James put it, *'resist the devil and he will flee from you'* (James 4: 7).

- Verse 12 – *'Put on then, as God's chosen ones, holy and beloved, compassion, kindness, lowliness, meekness and*

---

8   Acts 7: 51 – *'You stiff-necked people, uncircumcised in heart and ears, you always resist the Holy Spirit.'* 1 Thessalonians 5: 19 – *'Do not quench the Spirit.'*

patience.' Part of our responsibility as ambassadors of Christ is to show the fruit of it in our lives. We can only do this if we are daily walking in the Spirit Jesus walked. Our very countenance will then draw people to the Spirit of Christ that dwells in us. Paul described this when he talked about Moses who when he met with God, '*did not know that the skin of his face shone because he had been talking with God*' (Exodus 34: 29). A radiance flows from us because of the glory of the Lord and the Spirit that penetrates our being as we, '*are being changed into his likeness from one degree of glory to another; for this comes from the Lord who is the Spirit.*' (2 Corinthians 3: 18)

- Verse 14 – '*And above all these put on love.*' Love is the mark of those that truly know God and so John said, '*Beloved, let us love one another; for love is of God, and he who loves is born of God and knows God. He who does not love does not know God; for God is love*' (1 John 4: 7). We cannot truly love God if we are hanging on to worldly pleasures and influences.

- Verse 16 – '*Let the word of Christ dwell in you richly.*' There is no better way to explain the crucial importance of God's Word than to highlight some of the many things He says about it. The Psalmist was very aware of the vital importance of God's Word and so in a few simple graphic and pictorial words we read, '*Your word is a lamp to my feet and a light to my path. I have sworn and confirmed that I will keep Your righteous judgments*' (Psalm 119: 105 New King James Version). In the darkness of a sinful world the Word shines to light up the path we should follow. Its light also directs our feet to prevent us from tripping on any obstacles that may otherwise be hidden in the darkness. The wisdom of Proverbs explains that, '*the commandment is a lamp and the teaching a light, and the reproofs of discipline are the way of life*' (Proverbs 6: 23). Jesus took this point even further and made this incredible statement, '*He who has my commandments and keeps them, he it is who loves me; and he who loves me will be loved by my Father, and I will love him and manifest myself to him.*' *Judas (not*

Iscariot) said to him, 'Lord how is it that you will manifest yourself to us, and not to the world?' Jesus answered him, 'If a man loves me, he will keep my word, and my Father will love him, and we will come to him and make our home with him' (John 14: 21 – 23). Just as love for another person causes us to want to please them and do what we can for them, so our love for Jesus leads us to naturally want to do as He asks so that we please Him. We cannot help ourselves to do anything other than obey and this mutual love leads to an amazing unity – Father and Son make their home with us!

- Verse 16 – *'sing Psalms and hymns and spiritual songs with thankfulness in your hearts to God.'* The power of giving praise to God through song is sadly losing or has lost its way in so many churches today. The stage performance of a band and the types of songs they sing do not bring congregations into a depth of closeness with God. One leader of praise said to me recently, we do not have opportunity, with everything else we have to do, to spend more time than sing a few songs! What a sad reflection of attitude we have toward giving our time to God. We are missing an extra dose of relational power, lost because we corporately fail to come together in sustained, unified and meaningful praise. This is also reflected in our own personal time of heartfelt thanksgiving and songs of praise to God.

There is much we can learn from David. Fittingly, what we call today the Psalms was actually known in Hebrew as **Tehillim**, the book of Praises. It is not surprising then that about forty of the Psalms are specifically devoted to praise and the word praise appears over one hundred and thirty times in a book that oozes relationship with God.

Singing about and praising God brings release in our spirit and opens the door to the Holy Spirit. In the case of Paul and Silas this release was dramatic:

'About midnight Paul and Silas were praying and singing

hymns to God, and the prisoners were listening to them, and suddenly there was a great earthquake, so that the foundations of the prison were shaken; and immediately all the doors were opened and every one's fetters were unfastened.' (Acts 16: 25, 26)

Paul and Silas were doing what the Psalmist says, *'I will bless the Lord at all times; his praise shall continually be in my mouth'* (Psalm 34: 1). Prison and the constraints of fetters did not stop them! And did you notice, *'the prisoners were listening to them'* (Acts 16: 25)? Even those listening were captivatingly attracted to the joyful singing of praises to God.

Speaking to the churches in Ephesus and Corinth Paul also encouraged them to praise God filled with the Holy Spirit:

'be filled with the Spirit, addressing one another in psalms and hymns and spiritual songs, singing and making melody to the Lord with all your heart.' (Ephesians 5: 18, 19)

And:

'I will pray with the spirit and I will pray with the mind also; I will sing with the spirit and I will sing with the mind also.' (1 Corinthians 14: 15)

• Verse 17 – *'whatever you do, in word or deed, do everything in the name of the Lord Jesus, giving thanks to God the Father through him.'* It is in this verse that we summarize the verses of Colossians 3: 1 – 17 and remind ourselves that we are God's representatives through whom the world experiences God in bodily form. It is here where our renewal from worldly to heavenly transformation is clearly personified in and through the person we are.

Only the transformed can shine like beacons in a dark world. Only the transformed are seen by humankind as those radiating the inner presence of God. Only the transformed will walk in the supernatural power that will touch people as they walk nearby. Our wish should always be that we walk with God, so transformed that He is wonderfully glorified through us.

In these last of the last days, God is drawing together those that fulfil the calling of a transformed mind. It is through those that radiate the Holy Spirit that Joel's prophecy of the spirit touching all flesh will be realized (Joel 2: 28).

Transformation in our lives opens our understanding and knowledge of Heavenly things. It brings us out of the world in our thinking, speech, actions and behaviour and makes us Christ-like. It brings us to a point that just as Jesus prayed for His disciples and said, *'I have given them Your word; and the world has hated them because they are not of the world, just as I am not of the world. I do not pray that You should take them out of the world, but that You should keep them from the evil one. They are not of the world, just as I am not of the world. Sanctify them by Your truth. Your word is truth'* (John 15: 14 – 17 NKJV). So we too have been sanctified, made holy and set apart from the world to serve as God's precious instruments.

'His divine power has granted to us all things that pertain to life and godliness, through the knowledge of him who called us to his own glory and excellence, by which he has granted to us his precious and very great promises, that through these you may escape from the corruption that is in the world because of passion, and become partakers of the divine nature. For this very reason make every effort to supplement your faith with virtue, and virtue with knowledge, and knowledge with self-control, and self-control with steadfastness, and steadfastness with godliness, and godliness with brotherly affection, and brotherly affection with love. For if these things are yours and abound, they keep you from being ineffective or unfruitful in the knowledge of our Lord Jesus Christ. For whoever lacks these things is blind and shortsighted and has forgotten that he was cleansed from his old sins. Therefore, brethren, be the more zealous to confirm

your call and election, for if you do this you will never fall; so there will be richly provided for you an entrance into the eternal kingdom of our Lord and Saviour Jesus Christ.' (2 Peter 1: 3 – 11)

Food for Thought:

Jesus made a very revealing statement about our minds when He said:

'If any man's will is to do his will, he shall know whether the teaching is from God or whether I am speaking on my own authority.' (John 7: 17)

Chapter Three

Repentance and Forgiveness

'If my people who are called by my name humble themselves, and pray and seek my face, and turn from their wicked ways, then I will hear from heaven, and will forgive their sin and heal their land.' (2 Chronicles 7: 14)

Introduction

In Irish folklore there's a legend known as kissing the Blarney stone. The legend says that whoever kisses the Blarney Stone (Irish cloch na Blarnan) will from that day forward be endowed with pleasurable, shrewd and eloquent speech; an eloquence that the Irish call solabharthact, meaning to deceive without offending.

The origin of this legend is not really known but it's usually attributed to one of the MacCarthys, a large noble family from Cork. In true Blarney style, the details of the myth are really subject to who you feel is the most persuasive!

- Did the myth begin with Cormac Laidir MacCarthy who was believed to have re-built the castle at Blarney near Cork, Republic of Ireland? Legend says he was deeply entangled in a lawsuit and so in desperation he appealed to Cliodhna, an Irish mythological goddess and queen who told him to kiss the first stone he came across. Having done this he pleaded his case and won so, with gratefulness he took the stone and placed it into an outer tower wall of the castle.

- Or was Cormac MacDermot MacCarthy responsible for the myth? For reasons that are not clear, he agreed to hand Blarney castle to the crown in the late sixteenth century but constantly delayed its hand-over to the Lord President of Munster using his charming persuasive sweet-talk and alluring promises.

- Or perhaps it was Cormac Teige MacCarthy who was about to have his land rights revoked by Queen Elizabeth 1? The story goes that whilst on his way to the Queen he met an elderly woman who said, if he kissed a particular stone in the tower of Blarney castle his speech would transform into smooth eloquent persuasiveness that would charm the Queen not to carry out her threat to remove his rights.

- Or, is it an elaborate and highly successful lucrative marketing tool? Has a shred of truth linked the MacCarthy family, the owners of the castle, to a fable which has led to thousands of visitors struggling to reach the Blarney stone and kiss it!

Well of course the Blarney Stone is a myth, but it highlights a fact about this type of persuasive speech designed to deflect from truth that English colloquialism today calls the 'gift of the gab.'

The gift of the gab is the ability to speak with confidence, fluidity, gentle ease and persuasiveness so that people, often naively listen and believe what they hear. Having the gift of the gab does not always mean speaking deceit without offending. There is a side to this type of convincing, palatable speech that can lead to dreadful consequences; we have all seen, if not personally experienced this. Sales pitches designed to entice unsuspecting people into a web of deceit are such an example. But it can also be a sticky web of claims that a person may make in a job interview where they make themselves sound better than they are or claim they can do something that is beyond their true ability.

Worse still, are the smooth oratory skills in church sermons and teaching, which never really challenge or speak Bible truths, but lull the vulnerable majority into misguided beliefs. And what the speaker says is not actually true of their own life! What I am saying in this instance, is that there is a genuineness of faith that every true believer has a spiritual responsibility to walk in. There is no room for myths or persuasive talk that does not mirror the person we truly are in Christ. Yes, of course we are to speak in love and yes Proverbs says, *'A soft answer turns away wrath'* (Chapter 15: 1) and *'A gentle tongue is a tree of life'* (Chapter 15: 4), but these are for words spoken by those walking in humble harmony with God. I hope you can see that there is a very big difference between those who talk the walk and those that walk the talk.

The point is this; when we speak from hearts that are not right with God, we are like the person who is trying to look better than they are and making claims they cannot fulfil. There is a genuineness of character and holiness every Christian believer must walk in that will speak louder than words and so Paul wrote in his second letter to Timothy, *'Let every one who names the name of the Lord depart from iniquity'* (2 Timothy 2: 19). This departure from sinfulness is why repentance is so important and why we should fully understand what repentance is and why.

Understanding Repentance

Although I have said that repentance is important in the lives of all of us, people generally don't like messages on repentance. They would rather it was something kept out of sight and left unsaid. This attitude and way of thinking is actually nothing less than a mark of a person's sinful denial and ego. What I mean is this, there are times in all our lives where we have done something wrong but have not owned up to it. We have denied it or avoided telling the truth in order to 'save-face' and pride. Yet, the persona we depict is one of righteous living.

Masking repentance is a clever deception satan uses as he does not want us to fully grasp how vital it is and what repentance really means. It is why preaching about repentance is rarely heard and when it is preached, it often falls a long way short of some truths that, when revealed, will shake us to the core. It is these deeper truths that I will make known here.

The first thing every Christian should understand is that although the ability to speak with sweet, silky words may attract people and is socially esteemed - even to the point of bringing lots of friends and admirers, if we do not love as Jesus loves, we are as Paul said to the church in Corinth '***a noisy gong or a clanging cymbal***', in other words, what we might call today, all show but no substance, and in reality we are '***nothing***'(1 Corinthians 13: 1 – 3). This may sound harsh but let's also remember Jesus spoke these words:

'This is my commandment, that you love one another as I have loved you. Greater love has no man than this, that a man lay down his life for his friends. You are my friends if you do what I command you.' (John 15: 12 – 14)

The love of Christ in us is a command. It is a selfless, humble love that puts others first. It is also a love that if we do not have by obedience, means we do not truly love Jesus.

Without doubt this is powerful stuff and for some of us we might feel it is a step too far; a step we cannot reach. But, please do not be despondent; there is a hope, a revelation and a way and it centres on our precious Lord and Saviour Jesus who said, *'I am the way, and the truth, and the life'* (John 14: 6). So let's take a closer look at what is behind the command of love.

You might feel that I am about to go off on an irrelevant tangent but please bear with me as we enter some important revelatory experiences.

The message of John the Baptist was to repent and be baptized. Jesus took this vital message a step further and both spoke of repentance and proclaimed that the Kingdom of God is near, get ready.

Since both John the Baptist and Jesus spoke about repentance clearly it was, and still is, a key message. But why? What is really behind the call to repent and its plea that cannot be ignored?

Well let's begin by revisiting what we usually understand by the term 'repent.' When we talk about repentance today, the church has taught that it means turning away from sin or doing wrong. This definition comes from the Greek New Testament word **metanoeo**, which means to have a change of mind, reconsider, or think differently and was often linked to turning from sin. Indeed, this is part of what the Bible teaches but it is only part of a deeper meaning and significance. The first thing we must set straight in our minds is that we must stop thinking that repentance is simply about sin. In doing so, we miss its most important aspect, which is found in both the Hebrew language and Jewish people's experience.

The Hebrew word for repentance is **teshuvah**, which means 'to return.' But more than this, it is a word related to a very deep sense of regret. You see, the Jewish people were specifically chosen by God but they drifted away from Him. Repentance (teshuvah) is the personal recognition of one's need to return to God. It is the absolute determination to seek forgiveness and yield to God. So let's take a closer look at the implication behind what I have just said.

When John the Baptist was preaching repentance, he was specifically addressing his fellow Jewish people who had drifted away from God. John was imploring them to come back (to turn around or turn back) to their first love; to God. He was encouraging them to seek forgiveness for their wrongs against Him. To show they truly meant business with God, not just in word but in action, John publicly got these Jewish people to announce this by being baptized. Forgiveness of sins was subsequently part of the Jewish people's overall rededication to God and included the direct purpose of placing Him first in their lives.

These points were clearly expressed when some of the Pharisees and Sadducees had also come to John the Baptist for baptism. They were met by these strong words:

'You brood of vipers! Who warned you to flee from the wrath

*to come? Bear fruit that befits repentance, and do not presume
to say to yourselves, 'We have Abraham as our father'; for I
tell you, God is able from these stones to raise up children to
Abraham. Even now the axe is laid to the root of the trees; every
tree therefore that does not bear good fruit is cut down and
thrown into the fire.'* (Matthew 3: 7 – 10)

It is not a matter of words or simply going through the actions.
Repentance is about bearing its fruit of godly sorrow and grief (2
Corinthians 7: 10)[9]. It is about total submission to God.

When Jesus came, He immediately took the stakes higher by
preaching the gospel message; the kingdom of God close at hand. He
called the Jewish people to remember their first love and allegiance;
to forsake worldly ways, repent and put God back into His rightful
place in their lives before it was too late. Jesus was announcing the
last opportunity to restore a relationship with God. What I am
saying is the main reason repentance is so vitally important, is that
in truly turning to God, we are personally recognizing Him as God
and treating Him as God in our lives.

This is not a simple play on words; it is a significant mindset
change because when we only see repentance as turning from a sin,
our focus is on that area of our lives where we know it needs to
change. Our focus is on ourselves and we do it and then think, job
done, all is okay. Or worse still we commit the sin again and think
that saying sorry each time is enough. But none of this actually
places God first in our lives.

If we now see the entire picture, that the purpose of repentance
is about putting God in His rightful place in our lives the emphasis
changes, the commitment changes and the outcome changes. Sin is
now seen for what it really is; a direct and willful offence against God
and Heaven itself. Sin is now seen as the dethroning mechanism of
God from our lives. When God is not given His rightful place in
our lives we are floundering and lost.

---

9   2 Corinthians 7: 10 – 'For godly grief produces a repentance that leads to salvation and brings no regret, but worldly grief brings death.'

This all leads us to a crucial climax because if we do not realize we are floundering and lost without God in His rightful place, we know satan has worked his deceit and we have lost our love and become desensitized and powerless. In short, we continue to put ourselves first and remain wedded to the world.

To put this in another way, repentance is about running back to our Creator God, our beloved Father. It is about re-taking the place that we should have occupied in the family of God but do not for the disobedience and greed of sin. We are in this true sense, the prodigal child coming to their senses. This is why the parable of the lost son is so significant. We must come to the same point as the son came to; the point where he said, *'I will arise and go to my father, and I will say to him, 'Father, I have sinned against heaven and before you; I am no longer worthy to be called your son; treat me as one of your hired servants'* (Luke 15: 18, 19). Repentance is about recognizing who God really is and putting Him in His rightful place in our lives. It is literally about forsaking everything that is not pleasing to Him or bringing honour and glory to Him. This is why Ezekiel wrote, *'Thus says the Lord GOD: Repent and turn away from your idols; and turn away your faces from abominations'* (Ezekiel 14: 6). It is also why Samuel spoke these words:

> *'If you are returning to the Lord with all your heart, then put away the foreign gods and the Ashtaroth from among you, and direct your heart to the Lord, and serve him only, and he will deliver you out of the hand of the Philistines.'* (1 Samuel 7: 3)

The Israelites had wandered off into all sorts of worldly religious influences and philosophies, even worship of the Ashtaroth a goddess of Sidon. They had completely lost their way with God and the first three commandments were regularly being broken. God was no longer in His correct place and so the people had opened themselves to the destructive mercy of the Philistines who opposed God.

Samuel made two key statements about returning (repenting) to God:

He said, *'**If you are returning to the Lord**'*:

- *'with all your heart'*
- *'direct your heart to the Lord'*

Samuel's statement, ***'if you are returning to the Lord'*** is direct and pointed. The real question is, where does God really sit in our lives? Are we all talk; a showpiece? Or can we say:

> *'I through the law died to the law, that I might live to God. I have been crucified with Christ; it is no longer I who live, but Christ who lives in me; and the life I now live in the flesh I live by faith in the Son of God, who loved me and gave himself for me.'* (Galatians 2: 19, 20)

If we are not at this stage in our lives, we haven't repented. True repentance is about a change of mind. It is something that comes from deep within a person's heart. There is nothing superficial about it. Repentance is a total commitment. The whole point of repentance is that it is not just a change of mind, or heart about our wrongdoings so that we can tick a box or appease ourselves, but that we are doing it to return to God and walk, not in accord with worldly living, but in accord with Heavenly living. I cannot think of a better way to express this than in these words:

> *'Return to the Lord your God, you and your children, and obey his voice in all that I command you this day, with all your heart and with all your soul.'* (Deuteronomy 30: 2)

It might be unpalatable to hear but John wrote these sobering words, 'He who says 'I know him' but disobeys his commandments is a liar, and the truth is not in him; but whoever keeps his word, in him truly love for God is perfected. By this we may be sure that we are in him: he who says he abides in him ought to walk in the same way in which he walked' (1 John 2: 4 – 6). This brings us full circle to the fact that true love for God and love for Jesus will show itself in us because we do everything we can to please those whom we love.

The Mark of a Repentant Person

The recognizable mark of a truly repentant Christian believer is the loving self-sacrificial attitude they have toward God, which comes when they realize who He truly is. And in turn this realization and response leads to God's loving presence and power oozing from them and out to those around them.

The repentant believer walks in supernatural power because the supernatural power of God is at one within them. It stands to reason that if this power is missing from their life, they have not repented. Yes, you read that correctly, if we do not have the tangible power of God at work in us it is a sure sign that we have not reached the point of true repentance.

We witness this with Isaiah's experience after he suddenly became aware of God's awesome holiness. Isaiah, a man who clearly feared God suddenly realized just how unclean his life really was when he came into the holy presence of God. He immediately repented saying, *'Woe is me! For I am lost; for I am a man of unclean lips, and I dwell in the midst of a people of unclean lips; for my eyes have seen the King, the Lord of hosts!'* (Isaiah 6: 5). And on hearing the voice of God Isaiah responded positively and from that time forward received God's preaching and prophetic anointing power in a ministry that lasted over fifty years.

Repentance and forgiveness fit together in perfect harmony. As soon as we repent, God forgives us and this becomes the story of our lives because in turn, having been forgiven the costly debt of our sin, we must forgive. If we do not forgive, God revokes His forgiveness. This was the point behind Jesus's parable about the unforgiving servant in Matthew 18: 23 – 35.

A servant had a very large debt to pay. It was impossible for him to meet this payment so his master was going to take all he had but the servant, *'fell on his knees, imploring him, 'Lord have patience with me, and I will pay you everything'* (Matthew 18: 26). His master not only took pity on his servant but he cancelled the debt. That's the situation we are in with God. We cannot repay our sin debt but God, through Jesus has shown mercy and not only forgives us but wipes the slate clean!

Sadly, the forgiven servant met with a fellow servant who owed him a very small amount of the debt that had been forgiven and wiped away. What does he do when this poor fellow could not pay and had even, *'besought him, 'Have patience with me, and I will pay you'* (Matthew 18: 29)? The callous, forgiven servant placed his fellow servant in prison! Is it really a surprise that on hearing about this incident the master took back his kind gesture and made the forgiven, now wicked servant lose his privileges and have to re-pay?

Do we really think God will not punish us for our chosen disobedience if we act in an unforgiving way? Well, if you have any doubt this is what Jesus said, *'For if you forgive men their trespasses, your heavenly Father also will forgive you; but if you do not forgive men their trespasses, neither will your Father forgive your trespasses'* (Matthew 6: 14, 15). The word forgive used in this text is the Greek word **aphiemi**, which has several meanings, including to send away, disregard, refuse the release of a debt, depart from, leave as a friend or cause a difficulty. Forgiveness is about discarding something that is a burden, damaging or a hindrance.

What I am saying is that Heaven is the domain of the forgiving and forgiven. If there is unforgiveness in us, it is sin and sin causes a separation between us and God. When we understand these points in our heart and spirit we understand God's message of forgiveness.

Forgiveness

We can bring all the excuses imaginable to explain why we did not or could not forgive, but it changes nothing. Jesus, our role-model, having been beaten, spat upon, ridiculed and called a liar - hung from the cross at Calvary and said, *'Father, forgive them; for they know not what they do'* (Luke 23: 34). In these few words Jesus personified God's mercy and forgiveness; attributes that were not particularly uppermost in the mind and lives of the ancient world.

In fact they are attributes that have slipped away in our 'me first' modern world.

The arrival of Jesus and the emphasis of the New Testament changed all of this. What Jesus did throughout his life, and so dramatically in and through his death, was to highlight the open channel of forgiveness of sins and a new way of life through reconciliation and holy living. Jesus opened the door that reveals the true heart and nature of God and, as we have seen from the words of Jesus in Luke 23: 34, despite terrible persecution, pain and rejection Jesus was able to say, *'Forgive them.'*

What an amazing scene! Whilst hanging on the cross in excruciating pain and being mercilessly derided, Jesus selflessly not only audibly proclaimed perfect love but demonstrated it by laying down his life for us - that is, for both you and me. In this single act he granted to us forgiveness for what we have done as a result of our sinful nature. Put simply, he willingly and lovingly laid down his life so that we might have life.

Why was Jesus doing this for us? The words of John 3:16 spell it out, *'For God so loved the world that He gave his only son, that whoever believes in him should not perish but have eternal life.'* In both this Scripture verse and in Ephesians 4:32 (where we read the words *'be kind to one another, tender hearted, forgiving one another, as God in Christ forgave you'*) we discover that the originator of forgiveness is God.

In the same way that it was God who made the first move in forgiveness we as Christian believers must respond first to sins and transgressions perpetrated against us. It is when we are quick to forgive that the gospel message and the love of God are powerfully expressed to others. It is also a means by which God is able to work in unhindered truth and Spirit in our lives.

Put simply, if there is no forgiveness there is no Christian faith, and if there is no Christian faith there are no means by which we can reach the Kingdom of God. Forgiveness is the loving expression of God's heart. The Christian follower should imitate God's love and what He has done for us by living a life that is both forgiven and forgiving.

There is no point in any Christian believer going to church, singing praises, reading the Bible, telling others about the gospel message and then walking in disobedience by doing nothing themselves to put all of this into their personal daily life and practice. The truth of the Christian walk is not to look good and sound good; it is to truly be what we say we believe. This message is one of the central tenets of prayer.

Prayer and Forgiveness

The disciples of Jesus were well acquainted with the prayers of Old Testament people of God. They observed Jesus spending time in prayer with His Father and they also observed the miracles in His life. The connection was not lost on these men. Something was meaningfully different and so they asked Him how to pray. Jesus answered by saying:

'Our Father in heaven, Hallowed be Your name. Your kingdom come. Your will be done on earth as it is in heaven. Give us day by day our daily bread. And forgive us our sins, for we also forgive everyone who is indebted to us. And do not lead us into temptation, but deliver us from the evil one.' (Luke 11: 2 – 4 New King James Version)

This is a prayer that first recognizes God for who He truly is. It identifies the fact that God's name must always be kept holy in and through our lives. As part of this holiness pact, forgiveness both received and given, is then accepted as part of the agreement between us and Heaven.

We see a similar pattern in the prayer of faith in Mark 11: -25, which starts by recognizing the sovereignty of God in whom our faith rests and it ends with Jesus saying, *'And whenever you stand praying, forgive, if you have anything against any one; so that your Father also who is in heaven may forgive your trespasses'* (verse 25). Unforgiveness creates a blockage in our prayer communication. It causes a breach in our privileges. It stops us from receiving answers because it separates us from God. That is why we must obediently clear the blockage by forgiving as we are forgiven.

Obedience and Forgiveness

Forgiveness is about love, obedience and sacrifice. It is not dependent upon conditions or circumstances. Love expressed through forgiveness cannot harbour bitterness, anger, hate, resentment or revenge; they are opposite reactions. The logical outcome of this statement is that unforgiveness in our lives is a sign that we do not truly love God. Wow, what a powerful statement that is; but is it really true? Well, to find out let's look at the first letter of John where we read:

'If any one says, I love God, and hates his brother, he is a liar; for he who does not love his brother whom he has seen, cannot love God whom he has not seen. And this commandment we have from him, that he who loves God should love his brother also.' (1 John 4:20, 21)

And again we read in the same letter of John these words:

'He who hates his brother is in darkness and walks in the darkness, and does not know where he is going, because the darkness has blinded his eyes.' (1 John 2:11)

Darkness, of course, is the domain of satan who blinds our spiritual eyes and senses. Have you ever been in a place where there is literally no light? I had this graphically shown to me some years ago, as part of an exercise of trust. I was with a group of people walking through an underground cave. All of the torches were suddenly switched off and, literally, you could not see your hand in front of your face. We were totally blinded by the darkness and completely disoriented.

The point of this illustration is that hate, retribution and unforgiveness prevent us from seeing anything but the darkness of animosity, which envelopes us in its sticky tar of sinful resentment.

Now realistically of course there are times when we might be angry about something, but it is important that we balance our indignation or as Paul put it, *'Be angry but do not sin'* (Ephesians 4: 26).

In other words there is a righteous indignation or anger such as we saw in Jesus:

- Mark 10: 13 – 16 – Little children were being expectantly brought by their parents to Jesus to receive a blessing from Him but the disciples, thinking they were unduly bothering Jesus, scolded them. When Jesus saw what His disciples were doing, *'he was indignant, and said to them, 'Let the children come to me, do not hinder them; for to such belongs the kingdom of God.'* Although Jesus was irate with His disciples about their misguided actions He did not allow this to fester. He explained why it was important and then, in an act of love and compassion took the children into His arms and blessed them.

- Mark 11: 15 – 17 – When Jesus arrived at the temple in Jerusalem He found, instead of people in prayer and meditation before God, the hustle and bustle of a bazaar with its traders and dishonest money-making activities. Seeing this disrespect, He was righteously angry.

He drove them out and would not let anyone carry anything through the temple. But this was quickly followed by Jesus teaching why what was happening was wrong.

Jesus had good cause for His anger but He did not allow it to dominate what He was doing. You see, it is when anger takes control of our thoughts and actions that we fall into sin.

Paul realistically recognized that we may, like Jesus be stirred to anger over certain issues. After all, we all have a sense of what is right and what is wrong; of what is just and what is unjust. Our sense of fairness and fair play will be fully aroused; producing with them strength of feelings, but amidst all of this Paul went on in his message to the church in Ephesus to say, *'do not let the sun go down on your anger, and give no opportunity to the devil'* (Ephesians 4: 26, 27). When we are quick to repent and forgive we leave no room for the devil to play tricks with our minds. We instead act as obedient children of God and we do not hinder or grieve the Holy Spirit. It is for this reason that Paul completed his message about the moral standard of the church by saying:

'Let no evil talk come out of your mouths, but only such as is good for edifying, as fits the occasion, that it may impart grace to those who hear. And do not grieve the Holy Spirit of God, in whom you were sealed for the day of redemption. Let all bitterness and wrath and anger and clamor and slander be put away from you, with all malice, and be kind to one another, tender hearted, forgiving one another, as God in Christ forgave you.' (Ephesians 4: 29 – 32)

Forgiveness is a conscious and deliberate act of our will. Through the willing choice of forgiveness we unavoidably share in Christ's sufferings, but the paradox of this is that when we share in Christ's suffering we also share in the overwhelming abundance of His comfort.

Paul put it this way:

'Blessed be the God and Father of our Lord Jesus Christ, the Father of mercies and God of all comfort, who comforts us in all our affliction, so that we may be able to comfort those who are in affliction, with the comfort with which we ourselves are comforted by God. For as we share abundantly in Christ's sufferings, so through Christ we share abundantly in comfort too.' (2 Corinthians 1: 3 - 5)

In these three verses of Scripture the word comfort, comforts or comforted are mentioned six times as Paul emphasizes that with affliction and suffering those in Christ also enjoy His comfort. But what exactly does this mean?

The Greek word for comfort is **parakaleo** or **paraklesis** meaning to call close to or draw near, soothe, refresh, encourage, hearten and strengthen.

Forgiveness is not about allowing a person to get away with their actions or a person appearing to win unfairly; it is about sharing the burden of the cross, love and obedience. It is about receiving God's comfort and peace of mind. It is about being faithful, trusting and submissive to God. It is about receiving His blessings as we submit to Him and revealing the glory of the kingdom of God to others through our forgiving actions.

Forgiveness Exemplified

It is of course one thing to talk about lovingly and obediently forgiving those that have wronged us, but quite another when we come face-to-face with it in our lives.

I remember as a boy of about six years of age being bought a large ice cream by my grandmother. Walking some steps behind my parents and grandmother, I was enjoying the creamy taste. My grandmother turned to see how I was doing and at exactly the same time I licked some of the cream off my top lip. To my grandmother it looked as if I had rudely poked my tongue out at her, to which she complained bitterly to my parents about my wickedness and ingratitude. This small boy had no defense; his punishment was firmly sealed.

Unfortunately the saga did not end there. My grandmother, incensed by what had happened never really forgave me and stopped sending birthday cards from that day forward, though never forgetting my brother and sister. Many years passed and each time I thought about the incident, I used to break down and cry. Such was the impact upon me. It was not until my late-twenties that I understood that I had to forgive my grandmother and from that day the tears stopped. If ever the incident was suddenly brought back to mind, the Lord gave me peace and understanding. It was not my grandmother's fault; this small boy had done the wrong thing at the wrong time. The pain could have been relieved sooner had I realized forgiving my grandmother was my responsibility.

Truthfully, although this experience was heartbreaking and easily resolved, there are many people who have suffered greater things and responded with greater compassion and forgiveness. In some ways it is hard to imagine the suffering and pain they endured but met with love. Let's take a look at just a couple of examples:

- In May of 1981, the world was shocked by the actions of would-be assassin Mehmet Ali Agca who raised his gun and coldly shot John Paul II inflicting a near fatal wound. Time Magazine later reported that John Paul II embraced Ali Agca in his inimitable way and whispered words of forgiveness to him. But more than this, it was later discovered that John Paul II often visited his would-have-been assassin and even joined the campaign to have him released from an Italian jail so that he could return to his own country. When asked why he had forgiven Ali Agca, John Paul II simply said that it is what Christ had commanded.

What the Pontiff demonstrated to the world was that Christianity is not simply about what we say and how we extol Christ; it is about putting into practice Christ-like living in our own daily lives. As the world looks upon the Christian church it should not see a microcosm of the world, huddled together and being bold in words but fruitless in action and bereft of obedience and the power of God.

- This next amazing example of forgiveness took place in November 1987, and features Gordon Wilson (1927 – 1995) and his beloved daughter Marie who, whilst standing carefree and happy together watching a Remembrance Day service parade in Enniskillen, became victims of a terrorist's bomb. Still holding his daughter's hand when the bomb detonated, they were completely buried under a pile of rubble and Gordon heard Marie say she loved him very much before losing her life along with ten other innocent bystanders.

When interviewed about the bombing that had claimed his daughter's life, Gordon Wilson's selfless act of compassion was to express his forgiveness toward those who had planted the device. He also added that he would pray for them and pleaded that no one take revenge for his daughter's death.

The loss of their daughter devastated Gordon and his wife, but as Christian believers of their local Methodist church, they were eager to make certain that their small town would not be torn apart by the tragedy, but that the community would be reconciled and live in harmony with one another again. Gordon went on to work tirelessly as an effective peace campaigner.

- My third example of forgiveness features the astonishing story of Helen Campbell who tragically lost both her daughter Susan and her granddaughter Kimberley in what can only be described as an act of horrendous and mindless disregard for life.

Two young men entered the house of Helen's daughter and granddaughter whilst they lay asleep. As they broke into the house the young men aged nineteen and twenty were met by the two family dogs which they killed. They then went upstairs and attacked young Kimberley. Hearing the commotion, her mother went to see what was happening. The attackers turned on Susan and stabbed her several times. One of the young attackers exclaimed later that he did not realize that it was so difficult to kill a person and slit Susan's throat.

The attackers turned their attention again to Kimberley and she became unconscious; they then set the house ablaze. When interviewed some eight years later, Helen Campbell amazingly quoted from Psalm 119:71 which reads, 'It is good for me that I was afflicted, that I might learn thy statutes.' Helen then said that she wouldn't have become close to Jesus if she had not lost her daughter and granddaughter. Obviously still deeply affected by the atrocity, Helen said she hated the crime but she did not hate the criminals.

Helen explained that she wanted God to love her and, quoting from God's words, she went on to say that it is simple - if we do not forgive others, God will not forgive us.

Putting her trust in God she wrote to the two men in prison saying that she forgave them for what they had done and she also implored them to ask God's forgiveness. She went on to explain that she would pray that the Holy Spirit would let them know that Jesus died on the cross for them, that He loves them and that they need to believe in Jesus, ask His forgiveness and give their hearts to Him.

Helen said that she believes the Holy Spirit has directed her path. She explained that to live in unforgiveness is to cripple oneself; it prevents love and growth. She also stated that humility is the greatest act that one can take in life. It is a matter of humbling oneself before God and letting him take over.

When asked what good had come out of the tragedy, Helen responded by saying that it was turning her life over to God. Trusting God and obeying his command to forgive has not removed the pain of her loss, but it has lifted her out of the torment and shackles that unforgiveness otherwise offers.

Let us not fool ourselves; it does not take much to realize from these examples among hundreds and thousands of others that forgiveness is not an easy act. It is not something that comes naturally, and it often comes amidst great pain, injustice and even sacrifice. The alternative, although it rolls off our thoughts and feelings easily as we seek justice through retribution and revenge, is far more destructive and hurtful in the long run. That long-term damage and agony is greatest for the unforgiving person because sin is a destructive acid.

Forgiveness Removes the Corrosive Acidity of Sin

Forgiveness is about absorbing sin and reducing its impact. Paul writes these words:

'Now I rejoice in my sufferings for your sake, and in my flesh I complete what is lacking in Christ's affliction for the sake of his holy body, that is, the church.' (Colossians 1: 24)

What Paul is saying in this statement is that through his death on the cross, Jesus paid the final price for our sin. He took the sting of spiritual death away for those who will believe in Him and accept Him as Lord and Saviour of their lives. The result of this decision and personal sacrifice is that we enter the Kingdom of Heaven if we choose the life-long decision of giving ourselves to Him. But Paul also acknowledges that it is plainly obvious that what Jesus did not do on the cross was to remove sin from the world; we are still living in a sinful world and Christians will suffer just as much as anyone else from the acidic effects of it.

What Paul is effectively saying is that forgiveness is a means by which absorption of the effects of sin takes place. As Christians, through forgiveness, we take up our cross and place on it the painful effects of sin and stop these sins and hurts that face us from spreading their corrosiveness.

This act of love - expressed through forgiveness - literally binds the damaging effects that would otherwise spread like a terrible disease. Unforgiveness is sin and it causes strife. This keeps sin active as it bounces back and forth, spiraling down and getting increasingly worse as reaction meets further reaction. This ever-deepening, ever-worsening situation can spread and affect others. Even innocent bystanders can sometimes be affected when they meet a person's inner anger; it uncontrollably explodes, drawing them in as a result. Or they can also be affected when we react adversely in situations which are totally unrelated. This happens because the destructive corrosiveness of unforgiven hurts spreads. The hurts snap at the heels of anything that dares to cross our paths, thereby spreading sin further afield. The act of forgiveness sucks in the sin as it hits us instead of rebounding and causing havoc. It stops the thread of the sin, and in some cases it brings a person to conviction.

How another person responds to our forgiveness is of course their sole responsibility and God will deal with them in due time. We can learn to offload hurts to God through the avenue of prayer and love instead of bouncing them back through hate and making matters worse in the process.

The Ugly Torment of Unforgiveness

All the time we bear unforgiveness, we place ourselves in the prison of constraint that the sinful offence against us has opened the door to. It is worth stopping and noting this point again. We, as an active response, place ourselves in the prison called unforgiveness. The original offence has only opened the channel which leads to the door, but we make the conscious choice to walk into the prison through our unforgiving nature. Alternatively, we can side-step entering the prison through forgiveness.

Slipping into the channel of unforgiveness is in many ways a natural reaction to the offence because it challenges our sense of fair play and our notion of right and wrong. But unforgiveness brings with it anger, unease, separation, resentment, illness and many other disruptive and harmful elements that the devil uses to his advantage. In short, unforgiveness is sin. The only way in which these are totally relieved is through forgiveness.

Entering through the prison door of unforgiveness comes when we react in retaliation, spite, anger, revenge and resentment, showing no forgiveness or mercy and making no allowances. Once we are finally imprisoned, unforgiveness produces a merry-go-round of venom and hatred, which will never end if we do not get the unforgiveness out of our system and jump off.

We can find all sorts of excuses for delaying forgiveness, but these only serve to bind us; our hope, peace, joy and healing are held back. If we choose (and it is a choice we personally make) to enter the prison of unforgiveness, then the more we entrench ourselves in our rights, revenge, justice, hate and resentment the thicker the walls of our prison become. The thicker the walls of our prison become, the more we will become starved of freedom, peace and God's presence. What I am saying is unforgiveness creates a gulf of separation between God and us in that it affects our prayer link and relationship with Him.

In its wake, unforgiveness creates a block in the flow of love.

It also has a deeply profound effect upon our health and wellbeing because it disrupts the harmony of our body systems, creates disturbance of our brain waves and creates stress and anxiety. Recent psychological and medical studies associate this anxiety with health problems similar to those of chronic stress disorders, including muscle tension, high blood pressure and imbalance of body cells; these can lead to serious illnesses such as heart disease, arthritis and cancer.

What we are learning here is that our choice of unforgiveness has a direct impact on our physiological, psychological and spiritual health. It is a sobering thought that unforgiveness has a costly effect on us but often none on the perpetrator, who may have moved on, or has no idea how we feel, or may even have died.

The true loser in the process of unforgiveness is the unforgiver. Their health, spiritual growth and peace of mind are all compromised. The very odd and strange thing about unforgiveness, is that it is really a highly effective and destructive form of self-punishment. We will all know from even our comparatively minor experiences of a trespass against us that forgiveness is not always an easy step to take, and yet it is a strict commandment of God that many fall into disobedience over. Is God being unreasonable in His demand that even goes as far as to say that He will not forgive us if we fail to forgive others? No. Actually what we can see from all of this is that God is trying to save us from ourselves. He is trying to keep us from spiritual and physical self-destruction.

The fact is, God never said that becoming a Christian would be an easy way of life, but it is a blessed and fulfilled way of life. When we realize just how destructive unforgiveness is and how it cuts us off from God, we actually also realize that God is not being unreasonable in His expectation at all. In fact, there is no real choice to make other than to take the path of forgiveness. Forgiveness is the wise choice and it brings us closer to God.

It is true that forgiveness cannot change the past. The pain from past events, especially the loss of a loved one, will always be there, but we will never move forward unless we humble ourselves and forgive. Forgiveness can change the future.

Walking in Humility

In the Old Testament book of Micah, we come across some very special words that were specifically directed at those who walk in an active and vibrant relationship with God and who set aside an empty and hypocritical faith:

'He has showed you, O man, what is good; and what does the Lord require of you but to do justice, and to love kindness, and to walk humbly with your God.' (Micah 6:8)

The act of humbling ourselves before God removes emptiness and hypocrisy from the Christian faith and puts God in central place. We come across this same call to humility in the first letter of Peter:

'Clothe yourselves, all of you, with humility toward one another, for God opposes the proud, but gives grace to the humble. Humble yourselves therefore under the mighty hand of God, that in due time he may exalt you. Cast all your anxieties on him, for he cares about you.' (1 Peter 5: 5 - 7)

The call of Peter is to set aside self-importance, pride and arrogance and place ourselves totally under God's authority. As Christian believers we are all called to serve, be unpretentious, love, recognize God as Lord and allow Him to take total control of our lives.

The Christian walk is one of paradox. Jesus taught, *'if you lose your life, you will gain it'* (Mark 8:35); *'if you are last, you will be first'* (Matthew 20:16); *'if you are humble, you will be exalted.'* (Luke 14:11)

Humility is not about weakness and being trodden under foot. Humility is about knowing one's strengths and acknowledging one's weaknesses. Humble people will not promote themselves for gain but rather use their strengths to serve others.

The proud overestimate their strengths and deny their weaknesses. They laud themselves over others, seeing themselves better than they actually are. The humble person knows that God is Lord and that power and strength come only from Him. The proud person goes their own way thinking that success is born from their power and alone.

There is no cause for fear or concern about offering ourselves to God in humility. God will not reject or humiliate us. As we willingly sacrifice self to be broken and come in repentance to God, He will accept us.

Alternatively, if we are not ready to humble ourselves before God we will never see the fullness of mighty moves, signs, wonders and miracles of the Holy Spirit. These things can only be entrusted to those who know their place, who do as God commands and do not end up thinking of themselves more highly than they ought.

We should realize all is not well if the power of God is missing from our lives. Yet remarkably few recognize this or make the connection.

The strong tide of sin in our lives begins to weaken as we truly repent and humbly face God through the blood of our precious Lord and Saviour Jesus. When we forgive, we are not only unshackled from the bondage of hate and the destructive physical, mental and spiritual forces of unforgiveness, but we allow freedom to God to forgive us.

Repentance and forgiveness open a floodgate of love, reconciliation, peace and harmony between us and God, God and us, us and others. It is through repentance and forgiveness that the blood of Jesus covers us and the door of God's grace opens wide.

'For You, Lord, are good, and ready to forgive, and abundant in mercy to all those who call upon You.' (Psalm 86: 5 NKJV)

Food for Thought:

In 1896, during a revival in his Methodist church, Judson W Van De Venter (1855 – 1939) was overwhelmingly convicted by the Holy Spirit to give up his art teaching and become an evangelist. Although initially resistant to the call, Judson was deeply convicted by the words of Jesus found in Luke 14:33:

'Whoever of you does not renounce all that he has cannot be my disciple.'

Judson surrendered his life to God and was later inspired to write the words of the now famous hymn 'I Surrender All.'

Chapter Four

The Grace of God

'See to it that no one fail to obtain the grace of God; that no 'root of bitterness' spring up and cause trouble, and by it the many become defiled.' (Hebrews 12: 15)

Introduction

Many references to sheep owners or shepherds are found throughout the Bible from Genesis through to Revelation. As we look at these Scripture references, it is interesting to learn that some of the well-known or prominent characters of the Bible found their training as shepherds. Among their number this includes: Abel (Genesis 4: 2), Rachel (Genesis 29: 9), Moses (Exodus 3: 1), David (1 Samuel 16: 11) and Amos (Amos 1: 1). But more than this we also discover that Jesus is the Good Shepherd and church pastors are shepherds of the flock.

With so many references in the Bible to sheep owners, shepherds and sheep it begs the question, 'what's special about a shepherd and what can we learn from them'?

The Special Life of a Shepherd

The first special thing that quickly becomes noticeable about a shepherd is that there are three different types:

1. The shepherd owner. *'Now Abel was a keeper of sheep, and Cain a tiller of the ground. In the course of time Cain brought to the Lord an offering of the fruit of the ground, and Abel brought of the firstlings of his flock and of their fat portions.'* (Genesis 4: 2 – 4)

2. The shepherd children or relatives. *'Rachel came with her father's sheep; for she kept them.'* (Genesis 29: 9)

3. The shepherd hireling. *'He who is a hireling and not a shepherd, whose own the sheep are not, sees the wolf coming and leaves the sheep and flees.'* (John 10: 12)

The first two types of shepherd described in Scripture are what I will refer to as the true shepherds. The third type of shepherd, the hireling, is bluntly described by John as one who does not have the trademark dedication or commitment that the first two have. It is for this reason that John calls this person, *'He who is a hireling and not a shepherd.'* (John 10: 12)

The hireling is purely hired to look after a flock but they are not truly committed and when a problem or danger arises they flee and so John is really recognizing that they do not act and behave like true shepherds and so are not worthy of the title.

In contrast to hirelings the true shepherd's role was always taken very seriously and they diligently looked after the flock in their care. This included tending to the needs of sheep; feeding them, and helping them if they became stuck in thorn bushes or lifting them out of difficult situations such as ditches that they had fallen into.

Where sheep had injured themselves the true shepherd anointed them with oil, bound the wounds and healed them. If a sheep strayed the true shepherd brought them back and protected them from the ravages of wild beasts.

In fact, the true shepherd was so devoted to the flock that they would even risk their own lives to protect the sheep. We see an example of this selfless dedication with the young shepherd boy David who spoke with King Saul about confronting the Philistine army champion Goliath. The fearless David said:

'Your servant used to keep sheep for his father; and when there came a lion, or a bear, and took a lamb from the flock, I went after him and smote him and delivered it out of his mouth; and if he arose against me, I caught him by his beard, and smote him and killed him.' (1 Samuel 17: 34, 35)

As we read in one Samuel chapter seventeen, it is not long after the discussion with Saul that the young and fearless shepherd boy, David, proved his training, and with God's hand upon him, he selflessly placed himself in direct danger on behalf of his people and killed the mighty Philistine warrior Goliath.

David had not been tainted by the fears and doubts of his people or those of Saul. He was not discouraged by the taunts of the Philistines. He had learned how to apply his training and to trust God because the life of a shepherd was not only fraught with danger but separate from the rest of society thereby allowing time alone with God.

Although the life of a shepherd was occasionally solitary, it was also common for flocks to link together and groups of shepherds to work in unity by helping one another with feeding, watering and protecting the flocks. For example, when Jacob had taken his flock to the eastern part of his land we read:

'As he looked, he saw a well in the field, and lo, three flocks of sheep lying beside it; for out of that well the flocks were watered. The stone on the well's mouth was large, and when all the flocks were gathered there, the shepherds would roll the stone from the mouth of the well, and water the sheep, and put the stone back in its place upon the mouth of the well.' (Genesis 29: 1 – 3)

If these shepherds had worked in rivalry and opposition, refusing to share anything together they would not have been able to freely and easily access the water that was so badly needed for the flock and for themselves.

There would be little or no sharing and harmony. If one had a need, they would not have been able to receive support. Constantly facing danger and difficulties, shepherds knew how to survive and where to place their trust.

What Can we Learn from the Shepherd?

Just as many well-known greats of the Bible learned from their practical experiences as shepherds, so there is a lot we as Christian believers can learn from their example:

- The true shepherd puts the sheep first and favours them above their own comfort; even at the cost of his own life.

  In a parallel way, as a true Christian believer we are called to lay down our life on the cross and serve others. Our dedication to the Christian life is like the absolute dedication of a true shepherd. It is serious, diligent and committed both to God (father owner) and one another, those whom we serve (the flock).

  A Christian believer who has not laid down their life on the cross and fully dedicated themselves to God is like the hireling. When problems and difficulties arise, their faith wavers and they slip away or flee.

- The true shepherd will work in unity and harmony with other shepherds so that the flock is kept safe and secure. They also refuse to allow outside influences to hinder their work.

  As true Christian believers we cannot afford to criticize one another, speak badly about those from other denominations or allow influences from the world to upset or separate our walk with God.

If a Christian believer speaks badly about others, criticizes leaders and denominational differences and lives in what we have already discovered the Bible calls the flesh instead of the Spirit they are living like hirelings.

The true shepherd will look after the sheep, feed them, keep them safe, heal them and even go looking for them if they are lost or confused. To this end if you asked a shepherd what the role is all about, the response would be to preserve life.

The true shepherd will not slumber nor be complacent about his flock.

Isaiah warned us about the shepherds of the church who are complacent and slumbering saying, *'The shepherds also have no understanding; they have all turned to their own way, each to his own gain, one and all. Come, they say, 'let us get wine, let us fill ourselves with strong drink; and tomorrow will be like this day, great beyond measure'* (Isaiah 56: 11, 12). These pastors are not true pastors, they are hirelings who are scattering the sheep and allowing many to become malnourished and easily devoured by the latest fads. Their role as preservers of spiritual life is far from their psyche.

It is a tragic and sad reflection but we cannot always rely on our shepherd pastors and leaders. It may also astonish many reading this, but all of us, no matter who we are as true believers have a shepherd's responsibility to help, sustain, heal and support one another. This means that we walk loving, holy and supernatural lifestyles; a lifestyle that a hireling cannot live because the two ways of existing and thinking are totally opposed. But having said this, what evidence is there to say we are meant to live lives emulated by the shepherd?

The Shepherd In Us

I was always taught that the job of pastor is like the role of a shepherd and so it is something only done by the appointed pastor minister. Indeed, throughout the Bible this is exactly what it says about the church pastor. I have come to realize that this understanding is only a small part of the spiritual fabric of the church. I have also come to appreciate what being the Body of Christ really means and how it links with the loving shepherd-heart and flock.

Just as our own physical body is incomplete if a part of it becomes injured, impaired or lost, so the same applies to the Body of Christ, the Body of believers or flock.

When a Christian believer is not operating as they should, and struggling or slipping away from the Body of Christ, it has an impact on all of us. We do not function in the unified and supernaturally blessed way that we should. To rectify this, we must build the struggling believer up, bring them back to the throne, support them and if possible not allow them to slip away. We must doggedly do all we can to avoid losing fellow members of our precious family. It is not acceptable to simply let brothers and sisters in Christ slide away or to treat them as if they have an infectious disease. They are part of us. Everyone is as important as anyone else and that includes leaders. This is how the true family of God should live.

Although we would probably find this very difficult in today's society, we cannot escape the blueprint for the Body of Christ, revealed by the way the early church lived:

'Now the company of those who believed were of one heart and soul, and no one said that any of the things which he possessed was his own, but they had everything in common. And with great power the apostles gave their testimony to the resurrection of the Lord Jesus, and great grace was upon them all. There was not a needy person among them, for as many as were possessors of lands or houses sold them, and brought the proceeds of what

was sold and laid it at the apostle's feet: and distribution was made to each as any had need.' (Acts 4: 32 – 35)

We must all be like shepherds toward one another, living in united and loving harmony, caring for one another, and ready to give up what we are doing or share what we have to help brothers and sisters; determined that we will not let anyone go.

I wonder, did you notice from the Scripture verse in Acts chapter four that the shepherd heart and tenacity of the early church brought with it the shepherd nature of Jesus? Let's take another look:

'And with great power the apostles gave their testimony to the resurrection of the Lord Jesus, and great grace was upon them all.' (verse 33)

What wonderful words, *'great grace was upon them all.'* This also brings us neatly to the Scripture that heads this chapter, *'See to it that no one fail to obtain the grace of God'* (Hebrews 12: 15). Through these Scriptures we have discovered that the grace of God is something all Christian believers should get hold of and receive. In fact, it is more than this; it should greatly be upon us. But what does this really mean and how does it link with the shepherd's lifestyle?

Obtaining the Great Grace of God

When we take a closer look at the Greek translation of Hebrews 12: 15 we discover that it reads, **'Episkopeo me tis hystereo apo charis theos.'** Roughly translated this says, *'Take care of one another so that nobody fails to receive the grace of God.'* Wow! The life of Jesus is not selfish or insular; it is about taking care of one another so that we all receive the grace of God. And as we have discovered, the early church knew exactly what taking care of one another really meant.

The members of the early church did not just know what taking care of one another meant, they lived it. They lived the selfless, fearless, dedicated life of a shepherd toward the flock, the

Body of Christ. And this commitment was lovingly rewarded by God so that *'great grace was upon them all.'* (Acts 4: 33).

What we have uncovered here is a lifestyle of humility toward God and one another, which James summarizes in this way:

'God opposes the proud, but gives grace to the humble.' Submit yourselves therefore to God. Resist the devil and he will flee from you. Cleanse your hands, you sinners, and purify your hearts, you men of double mind.' (James 4: 6 – 8).

The background to this letter is that it was originally written by James to the believers of the *'twelve tribes in the Dispersion'* (James 1: 1) and it deals with various practical matters of the Christian faith. Because James deals with the practical issues of living a Christian life there is much we can learn and apply to our daily lives.

James reminds us that pride is a trait that God opposes. In other words, there is no room for the proud in the Kingdom of God. If we are going to receive God's great grace we must lead lives of humility, lives submitted totally to Him. We must resist the devil, cleanse our hands and purify our hearts. These are all steps that every true Christian believer must take to receive God's grace. But what exactly is grace? What is God actually making available to us?

Understanding God's Grace

The fact that we have found Hebrews 12: 15 speaking about God's grace and Acts 4: 33 talking about great grace seem to suggest there are different levels or experiences of grace. In fact this impression is enthusiastically supported by Paul's comment to the church in Ephesus where he says, *'But grace was given to each of us according to the measure of Christ's gift'* (Ephesians 4: 7). And again we discover a link between gifting and grace in Paul's letter to the Roman churches where he speaks of, *'Having gifts that differ according to the grace given to us'* (Romans 12: 6). And yet again, Peter also makes this point by saying, *'As each has received a gift, employ it for one another, as good stewards of God's varied grace'* (1 Peter 4: 10).

Clearly God bestows grace upon all of us but in different measure with some receiving gifting that requires more grace to accomplish. To put this in another way, some people are specifically recognized by God as worthy and trustworthy recipients of His increased grace. So if this is true, what is grace?

Well, when we turn to the Greek translation for grace we find the word **charis**, which refers to the overwhelming generosity of giving a gift; a good-will gesture that shows an act of love, favour and blessing. This favour and blessing is also something that brings the recipient into a place of joy, pleasure and a depth of love that causes them to speak with a genuine gentleness, sweetness and charm.

The Hebrew translation for grace is the word **chen,** which specifically means to show favour leading to charisma and sophistication of character. Grace is then God choosing to show or reward His favour and blessing toward and upon a person. The purpose and impact of this favour on the recipient is to bring them to a place of joy and charismatic or infectious love and sweet mindfulness, which Proverbs aptly describes in this way:

'The mind of the wise makes his speech judicious, and adds persuasiveness to his lips. Pleasant words are like a honeycomb, sweetness to the soul and health to the body.' (Proverbs 16: 13, 14)

These two aspects of grace shouldn't really be unexpected because they embody who God is. God is love. God's grace is freely available because that is who He is. He cannot help being a God of grace. To put this in a modern-day way, grace oozes out of His veins.

Why does He bother with us; sinners who have treated Him with unloving contempt? The Psalmist provides an insight into this question through these words:

'O give thanks to the LORD, for he is good; his steadfast love endures for ever!' (Psalm 118: 1)

God is so full of unwavering love for each one of us that He did not even spare His only and beloved Son from the suffering, indignity and pain He bore on the cross of Calvary. Why did He actually do this? So that we could have the price of our sin paid in full when we freely choose to take the option of turning by faith back to God.

This amazing act of love does not, as some have mistakenly thought, stop when we repent and accept Jesus as our Lord and Saviour by faith. As we give more of ourselves to God and walk in holiness and righteousness, Peter explains that we can, *'grow in the grace and knowledge of our Lord and Savior Jesus Christ'* (2 Peter 3: 18).

The fact is that much has been made available to us if we take what is on offer by living lives that are pleasing to God. We become partakers of God's grace when we freely choose to become diligently connected to Him. The closer our connection and commitment to Him, the more of His grace we become blessed with. In this sense what we become imbued with purifies us with God's holiness, and holiness becomes who we are to such an extent that we begin to act and speak resembling God-like attributes.

John explains these points in this way:

'So we know and believe the love God has for us. God is love, and he who abides in love abides in God, and God abides in him. In this is love perfected with us, that we may have confidence for the day of judgment, because as he is so are we in this world.' (1 John 4: 16, 17)

A classic example of God showing grace, why He does so and how it can even include others is found in the book of Genesis where we read, *'Noah found favour (grace) in the eyes of the Lord'* (Genesis 6: 8). This declaration came when everywhere God had looked He could only see the wickedness of people but in Noah He found a man who believed in Him, a man of faith and it pleased God. Actually we also find this sentiment expressed clearly in the New Testament book of Hebrews where we read, *'without faith it is impossible to please him. For whoever would draw near to God must believe that he exists and that he rewards those who seek him'* (Hebrews 11: 6). Noah was compassionately rewarded for his wholehearted faith in God. But there was more behind Noah's belief and faith.

As we read a little further in Genesis we discover that, *'Noah was a righteous man, blameless in his generation; Noah walked with God'* (Genesis 6: 9). What a lovely picture painted for us. Noah walked with God. That picture brings to my mind a happy parent – child relationship. The parent loving the child and doing all they can to protect and give what is daily needed and the child not only feeling loved and contented but also given gifts and blessings. A child so attached that they mimic the parent. The picture of walking with God is further enhanced when we discover that the Hebrew word for walk used here is **halak**, which actually means to follow, pursue, imitate and to live the same way of life. It was Noah's pursuit and longing to live in God's ways that brought him abundant blessings, even to the point where his family were also favoured.

Noah was a righteous man. He committed himself to God, pursued God and imitated God in his life. This is the call, the requirement placed upon each one of us in these last of the last days.

Talking about His return, Jesus told us to be watchful .He likened the days before His return to those of the time of Noah (Matthew 24: 36 – 44). The people were steeped in sinful living with no concern for God. Only righteous Noah and his immediate family were spared the sudden flood.

The days we are living in are like those of Noah's era. The horrors of sin are all around us. The pride of man has pushed God into the background and diluted the truth of repentance and humility. Be warned, Jesus is coming and He will only take with Him those living righteous lives; those that are committed and ready.

Just as Noah discovered, it is our act of wanting to live lives pleasing to God that displays His willing pursuit to favour and do good things for people by bringing us closer to Himself.

These points are again clearly expressed for us in these words, *'For by grace you have been saved through faith; and this is not your own doing, it is the gift of God – not because of works, lest any man should boast. For we are his workmanship, created in Christ Jesus for good works, which God prepared beforehand, that we should walk in them'* (Ephesians 2: 8 - 10). Here Paul explains that the activation of God's saving grace comes through faith. These concise words bring us to God's original intention. We were lovingly created by Him to walk with Him in perfect harmony and holiness. The blood of Jesus has been freely offered as what we might call today, a 'grace and favour' or good-will gesture offered to a faithful person.

It is because of the good-will of God that we are graciously empowered to walk as Jesus walked. It is because of the grace of God that we can pursue holiness. By the grace of God we have a doorway to salvation made possible through Jesus. It is a gift, it cannot be earned but it can and is freely received through faith. In fact this is the only way in which it is openly received. *'If you confess with your lips that Jesus is Lord and believe in your heart that God raised him from the dead, you will be saved, for man believes with his heart and so is justified, and he confesses with his lips and so is saved'* (Romans 10: 9, 10). It would be wrong however to think that it all stops here; thinking we have received God's gift and our sins are completely wiped clean.

A Word of Warning

It is not only worthwhile but important to re-emphasize a crucial point that I was making earlier when we looked at the example Noah set for us. Take a closer look at the last six words of the highlighted Scripture from Ephesians 2: 10, *'that we should walk in them.'* What we have is a clear message; walk implies moving from one place to another. Here we are clearly told that having received salvation; a spiritual rebirth and the honour of being the children of God, we are now to walk in good works. Salvation from our sins is one side of the coin; the other side is that we walk as Jesus walked.

How can we walk as Jesus walked or walk with Jesus if our minds and thoughts are not in harmony with Him? The grace of God is all about bringing us to Him and into the Kingdom of Heaven. It is all about daily walking in His grace.

Walking as I have already said implies movement and so standing still for a Christian is not an option. Each day is new. Each day is growth and each day is a pursuit in holiness and moving closer to God.

Many subtly misquote and misinterpret Scripture when they say, 'it is by grace that I am saved not by works.' The Scripture actually says, *'For by grace you have been saved through faith; and this is not your own doing, it is the gift of God – not because of works, lest any man should boast'* (Ephesians 2: 8, 9). God's grace in salvation is graciously available but this grace must be activated by our conscious act of applying faith in Jesus. The faith we activate is a living and dynamic faith that we must strive to maintain and develop. What I am saying is that although God's love and forgiveness flow easily His grace is not an excuse, license or 'free ticket' to carry on living as we have always done in our sinfulness and union with worldly desires and pursuits. To abuse God's grace is to openly abuse God and the work of Jesus on the cross of Calvary. Scripture in fact tells us about *'ungodly persons who pervert the grace of our God into licentiousness and deny our only Master and Lord, Jesus Christ'* (Jude 4). The abuse of grace is the denial of grace.

Let us fully understand, a day is coming when the grace of God will end. There is a time coming when God will call time on the opportunities that He has given. When Jesus returns, those that have not taken advantage of God's grace and walk in it, will be left behind. We cannot think that we can abuse God's grace by carrying on with our old nature of sin; thinking we can simply just say sorry only to do the same again.

Paul tackled this question by saying, *'where sin increased, grace abounded all the more, so that, as sin reigned in death, grace also might reign through righteousness to eternal life through Jesus Christ our Lord. What shall we say then? Are we to continue in sin that grace may abound? By no means! How can we who died to sin still live in it?'* (Romans 5: 20 – 6: 2). Repentance is the door to grace that must continually be left open so that all sin when committed is totally cleared. The grace of God goes further and deeper. By the grace of God we find salvation and healing. By the grace of God we become children of God and by the grace of God we receive the power of the Holy Spirit.

We must stop the damaging and costly thinking and teaching that says salvation comes by a simple prayer, which is enough, job done entry to heaven secured. In truth, it is part of the journey's beginning and not it's ending.

When Paul was eagerly invited to speak in Antioch's synagogue (Acts 13: 13 – 52) he reminded them of all the things God had done for their ancestors. How John the Baptist had preached a baptism of repentance and how Jesus had come to bring forgiveness of sins through His death and resurrection. Paul reminded them of the need to take heed of the message. At the end of the meeting the Jewish people begged for more teaching and insight. And we also read, 'when the meeting of the synagogue broke up, many Jews and devout converts to Judaism followed Paul and Barnabas, who spoke to them and urged them to continue in the grace of God' (Acts 13: 43). It is not enough for us to simply experience a one-off grace blessing, we must continue in the grace of God.

Look at what happened to Paul and Barnabas the following week at the synagogue. God's grace was freely extended to the Gentiles and many of them became followers of Jesus. Even though persecution arose from this point the account at Antioch closes with these words, 'And the disciples were filled with joy and with the Holy Spirit' (Acts 13: 52). They continued in God's grace and received more blessing and favour.

The Effects of God's Grace

The impact upon those that receive God's grace was embodied in Jesus of whom we read, 'all spoke well of him, and wondered at the gracious words which proceeded out of his mouth' (Luke 4: 22). This same gracious speech should come out of our mouths, coming from hearts that know the love and rich blessings of God in their lives.

In fact, whilst talking about graciousness in the speech of Christian believers Paul said, 'Let your speech always be gracious, seasoned with salt, so that you may know how you ought to answer everyone' (Colossians 4: 6). And again, 'Let no evil talk come out of your *mouths, but only such as is good for edifying, as fits the occasion, that it may impart grace to those who hear'* (Ephesians 4: 29). These are the hallmarks of true believers; those who are so connected to the Lord that they act and sound like Him.

The spiritual condition of a Christian believer is clearly seen through the grace, blessings, gifts and favour of God in their lives.

'Since we have the same spirit of faith as he had who wrote, 'I believed, and so I spoke' we too believe, and so we speak, knowing that he who raised the Lord Jesus will raise us also with Jesus and bring us with you into his presence. For it is all for your sake, so that as grace extends to more and more people it may increase thanksgiving, to the glory of God.' (2 Corinthians 4: 13-15)

Food for Thought:

'The Lord be with your spirit. Grace be with you.' (2 Timothy 4: 22)

Chapter Five

Living a Life Worthy of the Calling

'I therefore, a prisoner for the Lord, beg you to lead a life worthy of the calling to which you have been called.' (Ephesians 4: 1)

Introduction

As a teacher, I often said to my students, 'do not listen to those who say you can't or you are no good or you will never achieve anything. Everyone has a gift, ability, or talent; something that others do not have. It is not about can't, it is about can if you are willing to try.'

These words were challenged one day, whilst teaching some nine and ten-year-olds about how to become young leaders. I explained that the morning session would be about the theory of leadership and the afternoon session given to the young students to plan and actually lead an activity where they would be assessed by me for suitability to receive a nationally recognized award and lead small groups in their school.

One small boy came to me with the genuine innocence and honesty of a nine-year-old, looking rather concerned. I asked him what was wrong and he said, 'I am not very clever and I easily forget things I have been told.' I looked straight at this vibrant youngster and said, 'do not worry, I am not looking for you to get everything right after such a short training period, I am looking for you to try your best.' I will never forget that smile and the way he bounced away to prepare. Being concerned that others in the group might be feeling what this boy had voiced, I gathered the group together and explained that I was looking for them to try their best. I explained that there is no such thing as failure when you try. If you make a mistake it is an opportunity to learn, and to try another way and thereby improve.

I will never forget what happened next. A girl put her hand up and stunned me with this statement, 'does that mean the only failure is when we give up?' Wow, what a lesson in the power of the words we speak.

The Power of Words

As I look back at that humbling experience, I am reminded that in the Old Testament book of Proverbs we come across these wise words, 'From the fruit of his mouth a man is satisfied; he is satisfied by the yield of his lips. Death and life are in the power of the tongue, and those who love it will eat its fruit' (Proverbs 18: 20, 21). The fruit of what we say either satisfies or dissatisfies us and so that is why this Scripture goes on to say that our tongue has the power to bring death or life.

What we say and how we say it is so powerful that it can destroy or build and give life. This is as true of the words we speak to others as it is to the words we speak internally about and to ourselves. For this reason it is very important that we grasp the immensity and power of words and what lies behind the meanings that they convey whether in written or spoken form.

The words we speak, if we speak them often enough, can become what we think, how we act, who we become and what ultimately happens to us. To illustrate what I mean let's consider two true stories from my experience.

1- The Story of Wilf

I first met Wilf, a happy-go-lucky type of person, when he came to carry out some work at my house. Wilf was a lovely man who, as well as being exceedingly good at his job, had many interesting stories to relate. Although you would not have been able to tell, seeing him nimbly climbing up and down ladders, he had unfortunately suffered several heart attacks, which I only discovered when a trench needed to be dug through the heavy clay of my garden. He was willing to do the dig, but he said it might take him a while. Needless to say, I dug the trench!

About a year later I asked Wilf to do some further work, so he came one sunny summer Sunday afternoon to view the job. Over a cup of tea in the back garden the conversation turned to pensions. Wilf declared that 'with one thing and another' he would need to live to seventy-five before his contributions would pay back; he wondered if at the age of sixty-one it was worth continuing to pay extra contributions. He then said, 'Of course, I will not make seventy-five,' and added that his daughter had said he would die in his sleep.

I was truly alarmed by his frank statement and said to him that he should not speak and think that way. Wilf, jovial as ever shrugged his shoulders and on leaving said, 'I'll see you at 8am.'

Sure enough Wilf returned at 8am the next morning with his usual cheerful smile and completed the job by coffee time. I asked how much I owed and promised to take the money to him first thing on the Tuesday morning. With a smile he replied, 'You worry too much. You are not running away!' and with that gave a smile, a wave and drove off.

As promised, first thing on the Tuesday morning, I determined to get to the bank, and I walked to Wilf's house to make payment. Knocking on the door I was greeted by Wilf's son-in-law and on handing the money I owed to him he said 'Wilf died in his sleep last night!'

2 - The Story of my Dad - Fabian

My dad, a man I loved deeply, was a survivor of the forced and hard labour Gulags in Siberia during the early 1940s where average temperatures fell to -21°C and, according to some reports, even reached -55°C.

I remember when I was a youngster and my father (aged 50, a man of both physical and mental strength) moved concrete posts about seven feet long. We began by taking one end each, but to speed things up my father hoisted one concrete post over his shoulder as if lifting a light-weighted tube and smartly walked off. I did not wish to be outdone so I too grabbed a post while he was not looking and managed to get it across my shoulder. I can remember to this day the pain as the post dug into my shoulder!

Seeing what I had done and saying nothing, I watched with astonishment as my father proceeded to lift two concrete posts, one over each shoulder, and smartly marched off. Needless to say, I could not be outdone even if it was hurting. When my father came to lifting three posts, I gave in!

Even more astonishing (and I cannot to this day explain or imagine how) my father, aged about seventy, lifted his garden shed on his own and placed four old wooden reclaimed oak railway sleepers (which weigh about 180lbs each) under the shed to raise it up. He was a man who did not see a problem; he saw a need and found a way to meet that need.

After his untimely death from a stroke, I discovered that my father had often said, although never in my hearing, that he would survive until he was 72. He died in his 73rd year - four months after his 72nd birthday - a fit, active and strong man.

I cannot prove that either of these men had died as a result of their self-talk, but I can tell you that they got what they had said.

As we read earlier in Proverbs 18: 20, 21 *'Death and life are in the power of the tongue.'* We need to regularly remind ourselves that great harm can be caused by frivolous and careless words. A sneer or taunt can cut through a person like a 'hot knife through butter.' False and deceptive words can destroy hope and the poison of indecent words clings deep and produces toxicity and separation from God. The Holy Spirit will never associate with negative and destructive dialogue. Such speech should never be allowed to come from the mouth of a true Christian believer. In fact it is for this reason that the Psalmist said:

'Set a guard over my mouth, O Lord, keep watch over the door of my lips! Incline not my heart to any evil, to busy myself with wicked deeds in company with men who work iniquity; and let me not eat of their dainties.' (Psalm 141: 3)

The true believer's words bring life, love, comfort and encouragement. The pure words of Scripture combat falsehood, enlighten, restore and build. Indeed Paul was so aware of the power of our words that he included this statement in his message to the church in Ephesus about the moral standards of the church:

'Let no evil talk come out of your mouths, but only such as is good for edifying, and fits the occasion, that it might impart grace to those who hear.' (Ephesians 4: 29)

When we take a closer look at the original Greek translation of this text we discover that it says, **'*Me pas sapros logos ekporeuomai ek sy stoma.*'** Roughly translated this means **'*Let no unwholesome, rotten, corrupt or poor quality speech depart from your mouth.*'** That means swearing, harmful and corrupt speech for the Christian is as opposite as sin is to holiness. In other words if we do not impart words of sweetness, love and encouragement (grace) we are not only failing to communicate the true essence of the Lord but we are walking in a worldly and sinful way because our hearts are not right with God.

Listen to what Jesus had to say about our speech:

- Matthew 12: 36, 37 – *'I tell you, on the day of judgment men will render account for every careless word they utter; for by your words you will be justified, and by your words you will be condemned.'*

- Matthew 15: 18, 19 – *'But what comes out of the mouth proceeds from the heart, and this defiles a man. For out of the heart come evil thoughts, murder, adultery, fornication, theft, false witness, slander.'*

If these words of Jesus do not touch us and cause us to cry out, as the Psalmist did and say, *'Set a guard over my mouth, O Lord, keep watch over the door of my lips!'* (Psalm 141: 3) then we are not walking in holiness and in a way worthy of our calling.

The fact is, once received, words can draw out from within us emotional responses that may control or influence our thoughts and subsequent behaviour. The Old Testament book of Proverbs aptly explains that, *'A brother offended is harder to win than a strong city, And contentions are like the bars of a castle'* (Proverbs 18: 19 NKJV). No matter who we are, words spoken and heard (or written and read) affect us. Once they are communicated and received the sender cannot take them back. It is therefore truly amazing that although communication is a necessary part of survival and daily living for humanity, it is also potentially one of the most difficult and misunderstood areas of our lives, and as we have discovered our words are a potential source of untold conflict and harm. This is why we must walk in love and the power of the Holy Spirit.

The sobering thing about our speech is that as Christians, if we are not walking in love and in the anointing fire of the Holy Spirit, we are completely exposed to a worldly influence that can, and does, cause us to unintentionally convey the wisdom of man and false or misleading words and teaching. This is because we are not grounded in the truth of Scripture and filled with the Holy Spirit, who is our teacher, guide and counselor. What I am saying here is that many are speaking and teaching from Scripture but are doing so from a worldly perspective. It is impossible for them to do otherwise unless they are totally transformed and walking by the Spirit because spiritual truths and gifts are only understood by the Spirit. Paul explained this in his letter to the church in Corinth:

'The unspiritual man does not receive the gifts of the Spirit of God, for they are folly to him, and he is not able to understand them because they are spiritually discerned.' (1 Corinthians 2: 14)

It is worth stressing the point that these words were specifically written to the church where, like the church today some members were not totally committed to God and walking by the Spirit. Paul called these believers unspiritual, natural or walking according to the flesh.

The crucial importance of a committed and Spirit filled life is particularly relevant today because we have now moved to a time in spiritual history where the Word and Spirit must come together in God's anointed power. We are at a time in God's plan where the conjoining of the Word and Spirit will release a mighty outpouring of the Holy Spirit in Revival; a Revival that will shake heaven and earth. It will be a Revival that will spread worldwide; God's last given chance to call all people to Him before the final curtain of opportunity falls. But this will also be a time when many in the church fall away because the required commitment and intensity will prove to be too much especially as verbal and physical opposition grows and the cunning wisdom and philosophies of man draw those who do not hunger and thirst after God, astray.

Most of what we are seeing and hearing today are both the fruits of sin and warfare against God in the world and the subtle humanistic wisdom and the philosophies of man in the church that have been freely allowed to infiltrate and water down God's Word. Over time, the church has allowed the grieving of the Holy Spirit by leaving Him out, and in so doing lose the love, humility, gentleness and unity of the Spirit.

The speech of many Christian believers, when we listen carefully, is worldly and superficial. Superficial because the words do not match the actions or show the supernatural walk; superficial because the words are not kingdom words, they lack anguish and the deep desire for the heart of God that burns every waking moment.

It is very clear that we are constantly being bombarded by various forms of attack from our adversary. Peter warned us to:

'Be sober, be watchful. Your adversary the devil prowls around like a roaring lion, seeking some one to devour. Resist him firm in your faith, knowing that the same experience of

suffering is required of your brotherhood throughout the world.'
(1 Peter 5: 8 - 9)

The Greek words for sober and watchful used in this text are:

- **Nepho** (sober), meaning being calm, composed and collected or unruffled.
- **Gregoreo** (watchful), which means to actively pay strict attention toward and be cautious of.

There is no need for us to fear, worry or become anxious about the attacks of the devil so long as we are active in our caution and are taking the right steps to protect ourselves. Peter explained that we are more than capable of resisting and opposing the devil when we stand firm in our faith. Standing in faith means that we think faith, speak faith and act in faith and live a life worthy of our calling.

A Life Worthy of our Calling

We are duty bound to live lives worthy of our calling and that means we must stop all negative thought, speech and action. We say we have faith. And we also boldly say we believe, but the time has now come in these last of the last days when we must act in faith and belief.

Frankly, enough is enough. We must burn with a righteous anger over the destruction that sin has wrought. There is a saying that says, 'the best form of defense is attack.' Satan has had his field-day and dictated his lies to us but now is the time to rise up, fight for and reclaim what is rightfully ours because of the stripes, blood and death of our precious Lord and Saviour Jesus Christ.

Now is the time to heighten our expectation and turn the impossible into the possible because we have a God with whom nothing is impossible and we have Jesus who said:

'Truly, truly, I say to you, he who believes in me will also do the works that I do; and greater works than these will he do, because

I go to the father. Whatever you ask in my name, I will do it, that the father may be glorified in the Son; if you ask anything in my name, I will do it.' (John 14: 13 - 15)

These are powerful words spoken by Jesus. Since Jesus cannot lie what He says here is absolute truth. The qualifying clause is, 'he who believes in me.' That means every Christian believer who believes in Jesus qualifies! And all who qualify will do the works that Jesus did because Jesus said they will. All who qualify because of their belief can ask Jesus for the things that He did and whatever they ask, He will do.

Did you notice yet again that in these words we see the power of speech being heightened by belief; the power of asking and believing and the power of declaring our belief? Living a life worthy of the calling is a holy and supernatural life of faith and belief in our Lord. But there are also some other expectations placed upon us that go together with our calling to live worthy lives. Paul described these to the church in Ephesus:

'Lead a life worthy of the calling to which you have been called, with all lowliness and meekness, with patience, forbearing one another in love, eager to maintain the unity of the Spirit in the bond of peace.' (Ephesians 4: 1 – 3)

Let's take a closer look at what Paul said about the requirements of living a life worthy of our calling:

Lowliness

The first quality required to live a life worthy of the calling mentioned by Paul, is lowliness. The Greek word used in this text for lowliness is **tapeinophrosyne** or sometimes also written **tapeinophrosune**, which means to live lives of humility and modesty.

There are many things that we come before God on bended knee to ask and seek, but none are more important than to come to Him and ask that He deals with us in such a way that we become broken, humbled and surrendered to such an extent that He can freely work in and through us.

The Psalmist understood that the greatest sacrifice that any of us can offer to God, is our life and so we read: *'The sacrifices of God are a broken spirit, A broken and contrite heart – These, O God, You will not despise'* (Psalm 51: 17). Effectively what the Psalmist is saying is that if we are not broken by our selfish worldliness, the sin we see around us that separates us from God and creates the powerlessness that we experience in the church, means we will not find God's grace and walk a supernatural lifestyle.

It is worth remembering that God made this declaration:

'if my people who are called by my name humble themselves, and pray and seek my face, and turn from their wicked ways, then I will hear from heaven, and will forgive their sin and heal their land.' (2 Chronicles 7: 14)

This important promise from God hangs on the word 'if.' It is if we will subdue ourselves and come willingly under subjection to Him. And if we will pray and seek God's presence and turn from our wicked and sinful ways that then, and only then He will hear our calls. He will forgive our sins and He will heal us; that is, all of those who do as He asks of them.

This all comes together as a complete package. We do our part and God does His. It starts with us humbling ourselves, because if humility is missing we will never be able to break the shackles of self, ego and pride. And if we cannot break these rebellious restraints we will not live as useable and useful vessels for God or in peace with others.

Meekness

The second quality required to live worthy of our calling is meekness. The word used by Paul is the Greek word **praytes (or prautes)**; a term which goes together with humility and means gentleness, lowliness and modesty.

Meekness is a trait typified by those, who like Jesus do not promote themselves above God or others; they are mentally peaceful and serene in nature. They are slow to reach states of anger, irritability and provocation. There is an infectious mildness and serenity that ooze from those so connected to Jesus that His character shines through.

When Paul wrote his second letter to Timothy, he neatly outlined the requirements and characteristics of meekness in these words:

'Have nothing to do with stupid, senseless controversies; you know that they breed quarrels. And the Lord's servant must not be quarrelsome but kindly to every one, an apt teacher, forbearing, correcting his opponents with gentleness.' (2 Timothy 2: 23 – 25)

Instead of quarrels and fruitless arguments the outcome of meekness has the potential to bring restoration to a person and so Paul went on to say:

'God may perhaps grant that they will repent and come to know the truth, and they may escape from the snare of the devil, after being captured by him to do his will.' (2 Timothy 2: 25, 26)

Patience

Patience is one of the nine fruits of the Holy Spirit mentioned by Paul (Galatians 5: 22, 23). The Greek word for patience is **makrothymia** or **makrothumia**, which means longsuffering, tolerance, steadfastness, determination or perseverance.

Peter reminds us that if we do right and yet suffer for doing so, but also take the suffering patiently, we gain God's approval (1 Peter 2: 20). In this Jesus is our example:

'He committed no sin; no guile was found on his lips. When he was reviled, he did not revile in return; when he suffered, he did not threaten; but he trusted to him who judges justly.' (1 Peter 2: 22, 23)

The Psalmist said, *'Many are the afflictions of the righteous; but the Lord delivers him out of them all'* (Psalm 34: 19). And Paul, writing to Timothy also said, *'all who desire to live a godly life in Christ Jesus will be persecuted'* (2 Timothy 3: 12). In other words we are going to suffer for our faith but we are called to tolerate these persecutions and to persevere. Or as the Psalmist famously said, *'though I walk through the valley of the shadow of death, I will fear no evil; For You are with me; Your rod and Your staff, they comfort me.'* (Psalm 23: 4 NKJV)

In this modern-day of the diluted gospel message it may come as a shock to some, but we are regularly exposed to dark and difficult paths as part of our commitment to God. In fact Jesus said, *'the gate is narrow and the way is hard, that leads to life, and those that find it are few'* (Matthew 7: 14). Those that live a life worthy of the calling will know that the path to heaven is not easy. They know that the cost is great and many slip away but, they will also know that the suffering is by far outweighed by perseverance and God is always close at hand.

Forbearance

The essential quality of forbearance brings us to another key character trait worthy of our calling. The Greek word used here for forbearance is **anecho**, meaning to endure, tolerate or refrain and persist with in love.

Forbearance links together with patience and is best shown when a person refrains from reacting harshly when offended or when placed under provocation and acts instead with love and mercy.

The reason Paul outlined the character traits of leading a life worthy of the calling becomes clear as he explains their important outcomes in these words:

'...to maintain the unity of the Spirit in the bond of peace.' (Ephesians 4: 3)

- **Unity of the Spirit**

   Paul left us with this important declaration, *'For by one Spirit we were all baptized into one body - Jews or Greeks, slaves or free - and all were made to drink of one Spirit'* (1 Corinthians 12: 13). It makes absolutely no difference whether a person is a Jew or non-Jew (Gentile), male or female, slave or free, this denomination or that denomination, in Christ we are all members of His body and united in the same Spirit.

   Unity of the Spirit is about harmony and togetherness both between God and man and believing man with believing man. It is about unity in the church and walking in holiness and love.

   When we walk as Jesus did in lowliness, meekness, patience and forbearance, the worthiness of our calling creates a platform from which it radiates the soft unity of the Spirit.

   Sin, man's ego and selfishness destroy unity. They fragment, divide and separate us both from God and from one another. That is why divisions exist and the moral standards of the church are far from what they should actually be.

   It may not be particularly palatable to hear, but quarreling, hatred, disharmony, criticism and divisiveness are hallmarks of those that are walking worldly, unregenerate and unholy lives; disunited with Christ. Paul explained this point when he said, *'he who is united with the Lord becomes one spirit with him'* (1 Corinthians 6: 17). God is not divided and neither is the true believer divided. The Holy Spirit works where harmony and love flow. But where these are missing, He does not flow.

- **Bond of Peace**

All Christian believers are specifically called to live in peace and harmony with one another. This is why Paul wrote, *'we, though many, are one body in Christ, and individually members one of another'* (Romans 12: 5). Because we are members of one another, maintaining the bond of peace among all believers is a priority we cannot ignore.

There is no better way to summarize living a life worthy of our calling than Paul's words to the Christian believers of Colossae who were being constantly distracted by deceptive religious philosophical teachings.

'...put on love, which binds everything together in perfect harmony. And let the peace of Christ rule in your hearts, to which indeed you were called in the one body. And be thankful. Let the word of Christ dwell in you richly, teach and admonish one another in all wisdom, and sing psalms and hymns and spiritual songs with thankfulness in your hearts to God. And whatever you do, in word or deed, do everything in the name of the Lord Jesus, giving thanks to God the Father through him.' (Colossians 3: 12 – 17)

Just as the word Christian means a follower of Christ so we are to live lives that are fully pleasing to Him. This includes, as Paul said, that we, *'stand firm in one spirit, with one mind striving side by side for the faith of the gospel'* (Philippians 1: 27). This is the mark of a true believer who is living a life worthy of the gospel; worthy of their calling:

- Those standing firm in one spirit
- Those of one mind
- Those striving side-by-side
- Those walking in harmony

As true Christian believers we become one family, brothers and sisters who live in harmony. There is no division of denomination, creed, and colour, Jew or Gentile in God's purpose for us. We are collectively one Body of believers with Jesus as the head. We are all accountably entrusted as representatives and ambassadors of God to imitate the life of Jesus through the way we live.

Just as there is no division between God, Jesus and the Holy Spirit so no divisions and disagreements should exist among us. There should also be no criticism or fragmentation – we should all harmoniously work to the same purpose; preach the gospel and make disciples.

As we prove our reliability and rightly handle the Word of God with the help and guidance of the Holy Spirit, gifts are freely made available to us to build the church and promote the gospel both in word and action.

'And you, who once were estranged and hostile in mind, doing evil deeds, he has now reconciled in his body of flesh by his death, in order to present you holy and blameless and irreproachable before him, provided that you continue in the faith, stable and steadfast, not shifting from the hope of the gospel which you heard, which has been preached to every creature under heaven.'
(Colossians 1: 21 – 23)

Food for Thought:

You cannot enlarge your spiritual walk beyond the depth of your commitment and obedience to God

Chapter Six

Dare To Live Supernaturally

'I say to you, rise, take up your pallet and go home.' And he rose, and immediately took up the pallet and went out before them all; so that they were all amazed and glorified God, saying, 'We never saw anything like this!' (Mark 2: 11, 12)

Introduction

Who do you think you are? This is a question many ask as they delve into family history and discover more about their real roots. Most of us have an inbuilt fascination and inquisitiveness about our true roots; we seek an understanding and knowledge of who we are where our family came from, what they did, how we fit in and even what our purpose is.

Some people discover a lot about themselves either through research or families that share ancestry knowledge. Others, like me, know little, even to the extreme extent of not really knowing anything about their own parent's background. Others have no knowledge of their true parentage at all.

Often, a discovery of a previously unknown sibling or relative, or a newly discovered important connection with a celebrity are common identity disconnections which feature in societies worldwide. In this sense, there is an identity uniqueness crisis for many of us.

It was a treasured custom of biblical times and of the Jewish people to maintain their distinctive identity and background. This is why references to family lines are stated at various times in the Bible and why the Gospel of Matthew opens by painstakingly identifying the genealogy of Jesus (Matthew 1: 1 – 17).

All of this helps us to realistically put into words our personal identity and unique characteristics. It helps us to have a sense of belonging and to know our role, place and heritage.

For the Christian believer, it is particularly important that we fully know and understand who we are in Christ because it helps us to realize our true place in the family of God. It gives us a sense of belonging and appreciation of the full extent of the heavenly authority of the Holy Spirit that is freely available at our fingertips.

When I say that it is important to fully know and understand who we are in Christ, I do not mean this as head knowledge where we simply reel-off phrases such as, 'I am a child of God', 'I am secure in my belief', 'I have confidence in Christ.' These phrases make no impact on our daily walk and never bring us to the place of anguish, tears and longing but then we follow these by saying such things as, 'I would love to see people healed' and shrug our shoulders. I am talking about heart revelation that comes from total commitment and dedication; a heart revelation that produces open windows to Heaven and actions that support the words.

The truth of who we are in Christ and what is actually available to us was in fact concisely articulated by Paul in these words, *'I can do all things in him who strengthens me'* (Philippians 4: 13). The key here is 'in him.' It is our identity and connection with Jesus that makes all things possible for us.

When we know who we are and the full extent of the authority that has been given to us, we can command in the Name of Jesus against our evil adversary and then living supernaturally becomes as normal to us as it was to Jesus.

These privileges are not about my or your personal abilities, intelligence or status in the church. They are about Jesus in us. They are about the fact that we are children of God. They are also about our right to ask and receive from our Heavenly Father through Jesus.

When Jesus uttered those words to the paralytic man in Capernaum, 'I say to you, rise, take up your pallet and go home' (Mark 2: 11) He was speaking as One who was living the Kingdom of Heaven here on earth. This same life is at our disposal if we will recognize this right, have confidence to believe and allow God to work through us unhindered by our disbelief. We can because we are rightful inheritors of the Kingdom of Heaven[10].

If you are not sure if any of this is true, consider these incredible promises made by Jesus to all true Christian believers:

'Truly, truly, I say to you, he who believes in me will also do the works that I do; and greater works than these will he do, because I go to the Father. Whatever you ask in my name, I will do it, that the Father may be glorified in the Son; if you ask anything in my name, I will do it.' (John 14: 12, 13)

The words Jesus spoke here are nothing less than a true reflection of the standard by which each Christian believer should live as a daily matter of fact. It is the standard by which the true church should live.

The functional members of God's family know their place and who they are in Christ. They know their authority and crucially, they actually walk in it. The dysfunctional family members lack the deep sense of belonging. They don't know who they are, how they fit in or what authority they have and so they do not walk in supernatural power.

Dysfunctional Christians are like those under bondage. They think, speak and act like hirelings or slaves instead of living in the

---

10   Most faith teaching focusses on the words we speak. In fact Mark 11: 23, 24 is an example of this. But it is also who is on the inside of us that gives power to the words we speak. Jesus yielded everything to His Father. When He spoke He did so with the authority of someone living daily in the powerful Kingdom of God; a place where we too must live.

freedom of sons and daughters. Paul talked about this when he said:

> *'Formerly, when you did not know God, you were in bondage to beings that by nature are no gods, but now that you have come to know God, or rather to be known by God, how can you turn back again to the weak and beggarly elemental spirits, whose slaves you want to be once more?'* (Galatians 4: 8, 9)

When we choose to walk in worldly ways, or in what the Bible calls *'according to the flesh'* (Romans 8: 13), we wilfully and deliberately present ourselves to the bondage of satan's sinful domain. But Jesus said, *'Truly, truly, I say to you, everyone who commits sin is a slave to sin. The slave does not continue in the house for ever. So if the Son makes you free, you will be free indeed'* (John 8: 34 – 36). Where Jesus has set us free from the bondage of slavery and brought us into the adopted family of God, He has made us heirs of His freedom.

As heirs, we inherit the rights and privileges of Heaven so that we can do the same supernatural works that Jesus, our beloved brother, did. Praise God, great news, but why does this rarely happen?

Walking Supernaturally

The right to walk supernaturally in God's covering is something that we must fully grasp as possible in our thinking and diligently aim toward as Kingdom children. But if we do not think signs, wonders and miracles are truly possible for us, we will not seek after them and we will live and die bereft of these kingdom privileges.

What I am saying is the supernatural life of Heaven is a life every Christian believer should live naturally here on earth. Living in the holy authority of a supernatural life should be the norm, not the exception. It is a life that we not only can, but must, own by right as Christian believers if we live as true ambassadors of Christ.

Satan (because of doctrines of man), has tried to make us think we cannot live in the fullness of God's miraculous lifestyle.

But that is nothing less than an outright lie. It is the absolute right of every child of God and it is the domain of those that will humble themselves and crucify their lives with Christ on the cross. Herein though lays the stumbling block, the willing crucifixion of our lives, because all the time we want to hold on to even a small part of our worldly connection, we erect a barrier to the supernatural lifestyle.

No Christian believer can walk in the supernatural power of God unless they are totally humbled, broken and surrendered to the point where they can say these words, *'I have been crucified with Christ; it is no longer I who live, but Christ who lives in me; and the life I now live in the flesh I live by faith in the Son of God, who loved me and gave himself for me.'* (Galatians 2: 20)

The truth and crux of our inheritance is that if we are not ready to humble ourselves before God we will never see the fullness of mighty moves of the Holy Spirit, signs, wonders and miracles. These things can only be entrusted to the functional members of God's household who truly know their place before Him; those who do as He commands and do not end up thinking of themselves more highly than they ought, or abuse their privileges and become complacent.

It is when we proactively choose to live supernaturally with God that we move from living uncommitted worldly lives to totally committed spiritual lives. The sincerity of being committed lovers of God means that we will no longer live our lives, *'holding the form of religion but denying the power of it.'* (2 Timothy 3: 5) It is now that we can say with Paul, *'our gospel came to you not only in word, but in power and in the Holy Spirit and with full conviction.'* (1 Thessalonians 1: 5)

The reason this chapter is titled 'Dare to live supernaturally' is because it is about challenging readers to step out in faith or to put this in a modern way, it is about taking risks; faith risks in our prayer life, in our trust in God's word and our confidence in Him. It is about allowing ourselves to receive the Holy Spirit. It is about allowing the Holy Spirit to work unhindered in our lives and allowing Him to set us on fire for the Kingdom of God!

Jesus said, *'everyone who asks, receives'* (Matthew 7: 8). That is a very positive and uncompromising statement of truth. It is starkly clear, asking means receiving. In these words, Jesus was talking to believers and so when we come humbly before God, commit all to Him, and ask, we will with certainty, receive.

Now, perhaps like no other in these last of the last days is the time to take hold of Paul's words and repeat time and again, *'we walk by faith, not by sight'* (2 Corinthians 5: 7). This is a truth that must permeate our spirit, but what does walking by faith, not by sight really mean for each of us?

Walking by Faith

I have heard many Christians say things like; 'I will be healed when I get to Heaven' or 'my pain will be taken away when I get to Heaven.' In these or similar statements what Christian believers are saying is that Heaven will bring healing and relief. They are affirming their belief that this is what will happen in Heaven. They are making a declaration of faith in their future expectation of Heaven.

Of course, these words are absolutely true and correct. Heaven is the place of perfection but those that speak this way also demonstrate a misconception and misunderstanding that has tragically caused the majority of Christian believers to not only miss the richness of their inheritance, but also to fall into statements that say it is not God's will to heal even though Scripture does not say this.

Please let me take a moment to explain. We have all no doubt prayed this prayer:

> *'Our Father in heaven, Hallowed be your name.*
> *Your kingdom come.*
> *Your will be done On earth as it is in heaven.'*
> (Matthew 6: 9, 10 NKJV)

Have you ever stopped to think about the implications of this prayer and what we, you and I are saying each time we pray it? Let's take another careful look together at these words, *'Your will be done On earth as it is in heaven.'* Our prayerful declaration is for God's will on earth as it is in Heaven now! We pray it, sadly usually by rote, but do we believe what we are praying? If we do not believe what we are requesting in prayer, why are we asking?

It is a little harsh perhaps but when we pray in this way we are really praying 'in case' or as a rote prayer, a prayer of duty, but deep down we do not really believe the prayer will be answered, but in case God answers, we ask anyway.

If we believe that healing, pain relief and much more are our destiny in Heaven, and if we also believe we can ask God's will on earth as it is in Heaven, and we believe we can pray for healing, signs, wonders and miracles here on earth now, why are we holding back?

The absolute truth for every believer is this:

- God resides with us – *'I dwell in the high and holy place, and also with him who is of a contrite and humble spirit.'* (Isaiah 57: 15)

- Jesus abides in us – *'He who abides in me, and I in him.'* (John 15: 5)

- The Holy Spirit is in us – *'Do you not know that your body is a temple of the Holy Spirit within you, which you have from God?'* (1 Corinthians 6: 19)

- Jesus said, *'For indeed, the kingdom of God is within you.'* (Luke 17: 21)

Sadly we do not live in the full revelation of these powerful truths. Part of the answer to why we hold back is that we see Heaven as our home of destiny and faith where God and Jesus reside, while we view earth as the place where we temporarily live touched occasionally by Heaven. Earth is where we live by sight and feeling. Earth is where we are spiritually distracted and it is where we are really placing our focus.

By way of understanding these points a little better let's take a look at two examples of what I am saying here:

- John 15: 5 – 8 – *'I am the vine, you are the branches. He who abides in me, and I in him, he it is that bears much fruit, for apart from me you can do nothing. If a man does not abide in me, he is cast forth as a branch and withers; and the branches are gathered, thrown into the fire and burned. If you abide in me, and my words abide in you, ask whatever you will, and it shall be done for you. By this my Father is glorified, that you bear much fruit, and so prove to be my disciples.'*

  In these words Jesus reveals a precious truth that we must learn to walk in daily with the help of the Holy Spirit. During these last days living in the truth of the word of God and walking in the Holy Spirit is particularly essential.

  The truth is, if we abide in Jesus and He and His words abide in us, we will bear spiritual fruit. We will ask and what we ask will actually be done. This is the truth of who we are. This is what God says about you and me. These, among many other similar promises are the words of God that we must believe if we are going to walk in supernatural authority.

  The truth is, if God says something it is true. All that is personally required of us is to believe what God says. If we do not believe this truth the simple outcome is that we will not live in and by God's word.

  Whatever our past may or may not have been, it is in the past. If we are totally committed to Jesus and abide with Him we must do what Paul did from this moment forward; he made Christ his own and said, *'forgetting what lies behind and straining forward to what lies ahead, I press on toward the goal for the prize of the upward call of God in Christ Jesus'* (Philippians 3: 13, 14). Healing, miracles, signs and wonders are all part of God's plan for us here on earth. Paul said that he had to strive or strain forward. He had to press on toward the goal. That is exactly what we must do.

Whatever people say, whatever we see, whatever we feel that does not line up with God's word is a lie and deception. A lie and deception that is powerful enough to take our eyes off Jesus, thwart the truth and cause us to live defeated Christian lives.

Ah, some will say they are not living in defeat. The defeat I am talking about is the fullness of God and doing the works that Jesus did.

- Matthew 14: 29 – 31 – *'Peter got out of the boat and walked on the water and came to Jesus; but when he saw the wind, he was afraid, and beginning to sink he cried out, 'Lord, save me.' Jesus immediately reached out his hand and caught him, saying to him, 'O man of little faith, why did you doubt?'*

As soon as Peter fixed his eyes on Jesus and took them off the world he walked by the truth, freedom and vibrant life of faith. He was able to do what naturally we think is impossible, he walked on water! But as soon as he looked at the world (the wind) he became fearfully anxious (*'he was afraid'* verse 30). The Greek word used in this verse for afraid is **phobeo** from which we get the word phobia. Phobeo, in this context means to scare away, terrify or to become alarmed and anxious. It was at this moment that Peter began to walk by sight, which in turn caused him to sink.

In some ways it perhaps seems very odd that Peter had eagerly taken a step of faith and achieved something no other person had, apart from Jesus, but then quickly become fearful. Clearly this sudden change in Peter astonished Jesus who said, *'O man of little faith, why did you doubt?'* (Verse 31). It would of course be easy for any of us to think if we had had that amount of faith, we wouldn't have doubted. But the fact is most of us are living exactly like this. We look through the natural eyes of the world and at the hopelessness, our weaknesses and impossibilities instead of through the spiritual eyes of Jesus and the supernatural faith of possibilities.

Satan will always draw our attention to the natural world of impossibilities. He will always twist a situation so that we look at it through our own strength. In these situations we have to stand firm. It is not our strength that we are walking by. We have to see that the devil tells a partial truth when he says we can do nothing and we have no power of our own, but Jesus said, '*I am the vine, you are the branches. He who abides in me, and I in him, he it is that bears much fruit, for apart from me you can do nothing*' (John 15: 5). Because we are specifically grafted to the vine (Jesus) we can produce the fruit of faith. It is Jesus who does the miracle and He uses us to convey that power if we allow Him to act.

By way of illustration, in my twenties I was once asked to go with a missionary friend and pray for a man who was in hospital. He had suffered a massive stroke and was comatose. As someone who dislikes seeing anyone suffering, and believing in the healing power of God, I was happy to go with my friend and pray for the man.

As we were boldly praying, the comatose man suddenly sat bolt upright in his bed. He began to rise but at that precise moment I am ashamed to confess, my thoughts were, he has arisen, he is getting up and I became alarmingly afraid of a situation I had never encountered before. What was about to happen produced a wave of shock to come over me. No sooner had this fearful hesitance come upon me, the man gently lay back down and a couple of days later, died.

Think about it, if you reached a point of faith to ask for a dead person to rise and they began to move would you stay in faith or fall into fear?

Now this is the curious thing about what I have explained,

some Christian believers immediately bounce back with Paul's words to Timothy, *'God did not give us a spirit of timidity but a spirit of power and love and self-control'* (2 Timothy 1: 7). But they, some even with a hint of smugness, leave it there with no further action or response! This is because they know the truth as theoretical sight knowledge but do not live in it by practical Spirit knowledge.

The fact is, when we walk by sight we are not walking by the Spirit and we enter the world of fear, deception, sin and spiritual lifelessness where we see the world with its problems, difficulties and limitations.

In this world when we see healing needs we see beside them the impossibilities and all of this causes us to become fearful, doubting and unbelieving because we do not truly know who we are in Christ.

Paul made this awesome statement of truth:

'So then brethren, we are debtors, not to the flesh – for if you live according to the flesh you will die, but if by the Spirit you put to death the deeds of the body you will live. For all who are led by the Spirit of God are sons of God. For you did not receive the spirit of slavery to fall back into fear, but you have received the spirit of sonship. When we cry, 'Abba! Father!' it is the Spirit himself bearing witness with our spirit that we are children of God, and if children, then heirs, heirs of God and fellow heirs with Christ, provided we suffer with him in order that we may also be glorified with him.' (Romans 8: 12 – 17)

These words of Paul are extremely challenging and uncompromising because they clearly say, *'If.'*

- If we are led daily by the Spirit, we are sons and daughters of God.
- If we are sons and daughters we are heirs.
- If we are heirs we are not under the slavery of fear.
- If we are not fearful we also do not doubt.

- If we do not doubt we live in faith.
- If we live by faith we live in supernatural authority!

Walking by faith and walking by sight are like the opposite poles of a magnet, they cannot live together, and there is no connection between them.

Jesus asked Peter this question, *'why did you doubt?'* (Matthew 14: 31). That is the same question confronting each one of us as true Christian believers now. God's truth of who we really are in Christ is the truth behind our supernatural authority. It is the truth of a walk we can and should all be taking. It is a truth open to all of us if we will live by the Spirit. But what does it mean to live by the Spirit?

Living by the Spirit

If we honestly and eagerly want to live, be led and walk daily by the Spirit, God will honour our wish. This is not about trying to make ourselves something we are not. It is not about the false humility that says 'I have no right to ask' or 'I couldn't possibly ask.' This request is about boldly doing what God has planned for us, it is about earnestly seeking the higher gifts (1 Corinthians 13: 31) and being effective soldiers of Christ; preaching the gospel as it should be preached. Now that last statement, 'preaching the gospel as it should be preached' might cause some to wonder what it really means, so let's take a look at what the Bible has to say on this matter:

- *'..our gospel came to you not only in word, but also in power and in the Holy Spirit and with full conviction.'* (1 Thessalonians 1: 5)

- *'For the kingdom of God does not consist in talk but in power.'* (1 Corinthians 4: 20)

- *'..my speech and my message were not in plausible words of wisdom, but in demonstration of the Spirit and of power, that your faith might not rest in the wisdom of men but in the power of God.'* (1 Corinthians 2: 4, 5)

In these declarations, Paul perceptibly highlighted an issue that has, in many ways detrimentally affected and hindered the majority of Christian believers. Most of us originally heard the gospel message spoken by the wisdom of man and divorced from the demonstrable power of the Holy Spirit. This means that the gospel is understood through man's wisdom and in isolation to the power of God.

For example, many come to Jesus taught by man's wisdom, which says because of His love all they need to do is say a prayer and entry to the kingdom is secured. The problem with this teaching, is that the Bible does not say this anywhere. Yes, of course the Lord's love is part of the gospel message but the Bible actually talks about the necessity of repentance. This is why it was the message of John the Baptist and Jesus (Matthew 3:2 & 4:17). Repentance is about turning from our sinful and worldly life. This turning is not for one day or for a season in our lives but for the rest of our lives. In other words, it is about living a life of repentance.

This is why James said that we must keep ourselves '*unstained from the world*' (James 1:27).

The Christian life is about the total commitment of daily taking up our cross. It is about humbling ourselves and walking by the Spirit and in holiness until we enter the narrow gate to heaven.

The result of man's gospel message is that many settle on the belief that they cannot lose their new-found salvation; a salvation message that was initially based on man's wisdom. This inadequate gospel message can also lead to misguided comments such as I experienced from a church leader who boldly proclaimed, 'I am not interested in God's power; I am only interested in His love.'

As we can see the truth of the gospel is very different because the gospel message, the total commitment and the powers of God are not separate; in fact they are far from it. Our faith in Jesus is a faith of repentant love and power - that is what we were truly born into and why Paul said, '*that your faith might not rest in the wisdom of men but in the power of God*' (1 Corinthians 2: 5). To illustrate what I mean here is a bit like what happens with imprinting.

Imprinting is the bird and mammal innate drive to recognize and follow its mother from the first time it makes contact. Imprinting establishes within the new-born animal, a long-term behavioural response that means it will do what it is taught and follow where the mother leads. So a new-born duckling that sees a human instead of its maternal duck mother as its first point of contact will imprint on that person, learn from them and follow them instead of engaging with the normal cycle of a duckling's life.

In a similar way, as new born Christians, a parallel process takes place, we hear the message and immediately attach ourselves and our thinking to a particular experience, church, teaching or person. If the Holy Spirit, truth and the power of God are not a full part of this early process we develop separate from them. We then have to play 'catch-up' at a later time, if that time ever comes!

Meanwhile, the fledgling Christian develops with the Holy Spirit either partially or completely missing from their lives. In this scenario the power of God becomes something that is not known by personal experience and knowledge but by doctrinal understanding. It is for this reason that the gospel should always be preached under the ministry anointing and with the evident demonstration of the power of God.

In the New Testament Church there was little or no delay made between preaching the anointed gospel message, showing the power and love of God through signs, baptizing believers and experientially receiving the Holy Spirit.

The early believers were presented with a full and rounded gospel that constantly reminded them of their responsibility to live holy lives. If we are going to live by the Spirit there is an important issue that we must first resolve in our hearts. Paul described it in this way:

'The death he died he died to sin, once for all, but the life he lives he lives to God. So you also must consider yourselves dead to sin and alive to God in Christ Jesus. Let not sin therefore reign in your mortal bodies, to make you obey their passions. Do not yield your members to sin as instruments of wickedness, but yield

yourselves to God as men who have been brought from death to life, and your members to God as instruments of righteousness. For sin will have no dominion over you, since you are not under the law but under grace.' (Romans 6: 11 – 14)

Paul's powerful words bring us to a point of reckoning, which I cannot put better than Joshua, *'And if you be unwilling to serve the Lord, choose this day whom you will serve, whether the gods your fathers served in the region beyond the River, or the gods of the Amorites in whose land you dwell; but as for me and my house, we will serve the Lord'* (Joshua 24: 15). The question that Joshua is really dealing with here is, 'who are you choosing to rule your life?' Joshua highlights the fact that whatever path we choose takes a conscious decision on our part. The easy path is the world and living in the flesh. The harder path is the Spirit and living in holiness.

When we choose to live by the Spirit what we are really saying is that we will live a life that constantly engages with the Holy Spirit. It is a life that will do nothing until the Spirit has been given freedom to lead and guide. It is a life that is totally determined never to block the flow of the Spirit. It is a life that will not *'quench the Spirit'* (1 Thessalonians 5: 19). But what does 'quench the Spirit mean'? Well the Greek word for quench used in this Scripture is **sbennymi**, which means never to stifle, choke, hinder, thwart, suppress, quash or extinguish.

It is only when we are completely open to the Holy Spirit doing whatever He wants in our lives, that we will be in a place where He can fill us. But this will only happen if the foundations of our hearts are right and the ground or soil of our lives is ready to receive His supernatural implantation.

The Good Soil of our Hearts

The parable of the sower - or sometimes referred to as the parable of the soils - is found in all three of the synoptic (Greek **syn** meaning with or together and **optic** meaning see or seen so synoptic means see with or seen together) gospels (Matthew 13: 1 – 23, Mark 4: 1 – 20 and Luke 8: 4 – 18).

In this parable we learn that not every type of soil (a person's heart) is suitable to grow seeds (develop the word of God). Luke summarizes the key point of the parable in these words, *'And as for that in the good soil, they are those who, hearing the word, hold it fast in an honest and good heart, and bring forth fruit with patience'* (Luke 8: 15). In other words, the word of God (the seed) that falls on good soil grows strong and produces a good yield of fruit because the soil is ideal for growth. Well in a similar way the soil of our hearts must perfectly be ready for the Holy Spirit to take root and produce fruit.

This means that the soil of our heart must always be fertile enough for, *'love, joy, peace, patience, kindness, goodness, faithfulness, gentleness and self-control'* (Galatians 5: 22, 23) to grow and develop vibrantly into maturity.

These nine qualities are jointly described in Scripture as the fruit of the Spirit, not fruits. Let's explore why this is far from a pedantic point. When we compare this scripture with Jesus and the true vine we discover these words:

'I am the vine, you are the branches. He who abides in me, and I in him, he it is that bears much fruit, for apart from me you can do nothing.' (John 15:5)

We are the Kingdom vine branches. Just as apple trees only bear apple fruit and pear trees only bear pear fruit so the vine branches only bear kingdom fruit.

This point is meaningfully important because they are qualities that those who live and walk by the Spirit will not only show in their lives but they will show them in their entirety. You see, where the Holy Spirit is in a person's daily life it is not a matter of one or two of these qualities in evidence, it is all of them. In turn, these points are important because the fruit of the Spirit describe the character and person of the Holy Spirit who is gentle and easily grieved.

Where there is a lack of these qualities in a person's life, or sensitivity in a gathering of Christian believers, the Holy Spirit will not manifest Himself. We have to learn that peace and gentleness are necessary for the Spirit to flow.

Unfortunately many Christian believers do not know the Holy Spirit and so they do not understand Him or recognize the difference between spiritual hype and spiritual reality.

Often modern-day Christian believers mistake the presence of the Holy Spirit because they have been brought up to engage in a spiritual hype that whips them up like cream in a pressurized can that quickly reduces to a pool of liquid lacking substance and perfection. Satan is not threatened by these situations and so he is content to allow them to placate those in such meetings.

The clue behind knowing the actual presence of the Holy Spirit is in His title, Holy. The true evidence of the Holy Spirit is distinctive, perfect, lasting and gently powerful because His gifts are supernaturally visible and bring glory to God. Evil spirits have to flee and peace flows. So if all of this is available to us how can we receive them?

How to Receive the Holy Spirit

In His discourse on prayer Jesus closed with these words, *'If you then, who are evil, know how to give good gifts to your children, how much more will the heavenly Father give the Holy Spirit to those who ask him!'* (Luke 11: 13). It is clear from these words of Jesus that we must come to such a point of need in our lives that we ask God for the Holy Spirit. It should always be our prayer that the Holy Spirit comes on us and on the church. But in our asking, as I have already mentioned, we must also know how to work together with the Holy Spirit. And part of that cooperation with the Holy Spirit is a willingness to pay the price.

To give an example of what I mean about being willing to pay the price, I think it is worth repeating the unforgettable meeting that I had with God a few years ago, where I found myself not just talking with the Lord but literally shouting out to Him; calling out for more in my Christian life and with tears of anguish giving to Him my heart, mind, body, spirit and soul.

I thought that I had done all I could but God literally stopped me in my tracks and asked me this simple question – 'whatever it costs?' There was no price tag; it was an all or nothing question. The point is, if we truly want the fire of the Holy Spirit we have to also be willing to pay the price. The question is 'how hungry and thirsty are we?'

Hunger and Thirst

Those who experienced life in Concentration camps and Gulags or even those who live on the streets have been known to eat potato peels, bread mixed with sawdust and waste taken from garbage bins. Some have taken food from dead people and have in desperation eaten rats! The thirsty will drink muddy water or even their urine! Why? Because when we are truly physically hungry and thirsty we will eat and drink anything to survive. We will seek to gratify our hunger and thirst to the point of doing whatever is necessary, or giving all we have for one meal, just as Esau did when he gave his birth-right away for a single pottage of lentils (Genesis 25: 27 – 34).

In a similar way, if our spiritual hunger and thirst for more of God does not percolate in a bubbling desperation through our hearts and spirit, then something is wrong with our commitment and relationship with God.

A Christian believer that lacks hunger and thirst for God does not seek more from Him; they are content with what they have and are unwilling to humble themselves, by giving all of themselves to God. Sadly those who fall into this category will never know the fullness of His intentions, because they choose to stop short of receiving it.

Let's take a look at what Jesus said:

'Truly, truly, I say to you, unless a grain of wheat falls into the earth and dies, it remains alone; but if it dies, it bears much fruit. He who loves his life loses it, and he who hates his life in this world will keep it for eternal life. If any one serves me, he must follow me; and where I am, there shall my servant be also;

if any one serves me, the Father will honour him.' (John 12: 24 – 26)

The paradox of Scripture is that we die to live. We give up our rights to take up the Lord's rights. We submit to conquer. The more we surrender to God the hungrier and thirstier we become. The greater our hunger and thirst become the more we surrender of self and the easier it is for God to work through us.

Paul summarized these points when he said:

'If then you have been raised with Christ, seek the things that are above, where Christ is, seated at the right hand of God. Set your minds on things that are above, not on things that are on earth. For you have died, and your life is hid with Christ in God. When Christ who is our life appears, then you also will appear with him in glory.' (Colossians 3: 1 – 4)

If we have truly died to self and nailed ourselves firmly to the cross our focus will concentrate on the righteousness of Heaven. Our whole motivation will seek to conform to God's will. Or to put this in another way, we will hunger and thirst after righteousness. This is why when Jesus was delivering what we now call the Sermon on the Mount, He said:

'Blessed are those who hunger and thirst for righteousness sake, for they shall be satisfied.' (Matthew 5: 5)

What a positive statement, we 'shall be satisfied'! In these few simple words we have the absolute assurance that our hunger and thirst for the righteousness of God will always be totally satisfied. There is no better time than now to act on the words of Jesus. This is the time to go boldly and confidently in search of God, to call into the heart of Heaven with everything we have until with all our might, we grasp and take a firm hold of God and God meets with us.

We come across an example of the burning desperation for God that I am talking about with the Psalmist whom we would probably describe today as a person who 'wears his heart on his sleeve' and who called out:

'O God, You are my God; Early will I seek You; My soul thirsts for You; My flesh longs for You In a dry and thirsty land Where there is no water.' (Psalm 63:1 NKJV)

I guess it is true that few of us have experienced what it is like to really be desperate for water to quench our thirst, but we may have been thirsty enough to gulp down a glass of water with one tilt back of the head, only to repeat the process. Or we may have observed a thirsty animal drinking from water, just as the Psalmist did when he equated his longing for God with that of a thirsty deer:

'As the deer pants for the water brooks, So pants my soul for You, O God. My soul thirsts for God, for the living God. When shall I come and appear before God? My tears have been my food day and night.' (Psalm 42: 1 – 3 NKJV)

These words of the Psalmist are illustrative of a deeply passionate need, a longing, desperation or a drive for satisfaction – a drive so powerful that it consumes the person in their search and longing. Those that have taken this journey will know all too well that this drive is so potent that it causes them to focus intently in one direction, even to shout out to God and be willing to give anything to be satisfied.

The inner desperation of a soul seeking God's face brings inner pain and anguish along with weeping; it is most certainly not a journey taken lightly or easily but the end is holy satisfaction and release.

The thing about thirsting for God and being hungry for more of what He offers is that we first need to have a wilderness experience in our lives and to *'taste and see that the Lord is good'* (Psalm 34: 8). We need to realize that we will never be satisfied until we enjoy a closer walk with God in our lives. To know Him, not in theory but in a day-to-day relationship, is a point in our walk with God where we will be truly satisfied and delivered.

Spiritually, all of this leaves us with a question that we should face in our Christian lives and that is, 'what do we want most of all from our life with Christ?' No greater longing in us should exist that is not the yearning to do the will of God. To do the will of God we need the Holy Spirit.

At various key times in Scripture the Holy Spirit revealed Himself. For example:

- Matthew 1: 18 – *'Now the birth of Jesus Christ took place in this way. When his mother Mary had been betrothed to Joseph, before they came together she was found to be with child of the Holy Spirit.'*

- Matthew 3: 16 – *'And when Jesus was baptized, he went up immediately from the water, and behold, the heavens were opened and he saw the Spirit of God descending like a dove, and alighting on him.'*

- Acts 2: 2 – 4 – *'And suddenly a sound came from heaven like the rush of a mighty wind, and it filled all the house where they were sitting. And there appeared to them tongues as of fire, distributed and resting on each of them. And they were all filled with the Holy Spirit and began to speak in other tongues, as the Spirit gave them utterance.'*

Jesus said, *'it is to your advantage that I go away, for if I do not go away, the Counselor will not come to you'* (John 16: 7). When the Holy Spirit came He transformed the lives He touched. That was true in Scripture and it is also true of the lives of those who have wonderfully been touched by His fire throughout history; including times of revival.

The early church knew by tangible experience of the presence and power of the Holy Spirit in a way that has all but been lost to us today - that is why we read, *'Now the company of those that believed were of one heart and soul, and no one said that any of the things which he possessed was his own, but they had everything in common. And with great power the apostles gave their testimony to the resurrection of the Lord Jesus, and great grace was upon them all'* (Acts 4: 32, 33). These early believers knew **'great power'** and **'great grace'**! How many of us today can truly say we know great power and great grace? We may have lost this, but we can also restore it if we are truly willing and determined to do whatever it takes spiritually.

David was so reliant on the Holy Spirit that he pleaded with God; '*Do not cast me away from Your presence, And do not take Your Holy Spirit from me*' (Psalm 51: 11 NKJV). It is this reliance that we must hunger and thirst after if we are to move in the supernatural lifestyle that God intends for us. But David's experience also prompts two other crucial points:

1.   How do we know if we have truly surrendered to the Holy Spirit?[11] The answer is simply stated in these words. '*You shall receive power when the Holy Spirit comes upon you*' (Acts 1: 8). In other words, if we are truly walking with and in the Holy Spirit we will also be endowed with power.

2.   Can we lose the Holy Spirit? David was clearly aware of the possibility when he pleaded; '*do not take Your Holy Spirit from me*' (Psalm 51: 11). But also we know from Paul's words that it is possible to quench the Holy Spirit (1 Thessalonians 5: 19) and grieve Him (Ephesians 4: 30).

It is of course not in the devil's interest that we should understand our real need to walk in the supernatural power of the Holy Spirit. But if we could grasp how much we need the Holy Spirit in our lives it would transform our approach and attitude toward Him and transform our entire Christian walk because the possibilities of God will be unleashed and shake Heaven and earth.

Walking in the Possibilities of God

When we walk in the possibilities of God we walk in the immeasurable opportunities that bring glory to His name and souls to the kingdom.

---

11   Surrendering to the Holy Spirit means that He must have the freedom to take control of our lives. Once we have learned to walk in love and fully yield our hearts to Him we begin an awesome journey where we will walk daily and progress both with and in the Spirit. The loving unity of our heart and life in the Spirit will release His power.

Walking in the possibilities of God is so immense that the angel Gabriel said, *'For with God nothing will be impossible'* (Luke 1: 37). That is a core truth that we must fully grasp if we are going to reach our true potential. God, our Creator, has supreme control and power and so, just as He did with Paul so He will do with us; *'God did extraordinary miracles by the hands of Paul, so that handkerchiefs or aprons were carried away from his body to the sick, and diseases left them and the evil spirits came out of them'* (Acts 19: 11, 12).

The plain fact is this, it is God's will to empower us but we must first get into His will. We must hear His call and respond to it by faith, which is, *'the assurance of things hoped for, the conviction of things not seen'* (Hebrews 11: 1). It is when we have that assurance and conviction that fear, uncertainty, doubt, hesitation and timidity depart from us. Not because we are able, but because He is able.

The point I am making is clearly illustrated by the testing experience of the people of Israel after Pharaoh had eventually let them leave Egypt (Exodus chapter 14). Having made his decision, Pharaoh changed his mind and started to chase after the Israelites. As soon as the people saw Pharaoh approaching they became fearful and started to say that they would have been better off staying under Egyptian slavery. But Moses said, *'Fear not, stand firm, and see the salvation of the Lord, which he will work for you today'* (Exodus 14: 13). The people fell into fear and began to distrust God and even began to say they would have been better off as they were! But Moses stepped in and called the people to stand firm or as Paul put it, *'having done all, to stand'* (Ephesians 6: 13). The standing firm here is about immovably sticking to our ground of faith. But we then read that the people and Moses cried out to God; a cry that brought this reaction from Him, *'Why do you cry to me? Tell the people of Israel to go forward'* (Exodus 14: 15). This teaches us that instead of freezing like a rabbit in headlights when confronted with a challenge and being inactive in our faith we must get up, move forward, put our belief into practice and use the gifts of the Spirit.

We come across an example of standing firm in faith and exercising it in the incident involving Jairus' daughter. Jairus came to Jesus seeking her healing but whilst speaking news arrived that the twelve-year-old had died. *'But Jesus on hearing this answered him, 'Do not fear, only believe, and she shall be well'* (Luke 8: 50). In just those few powerful words Jesus taught us a precious heavenly family truth, *'**believe**.'*

When we make excuses for why something we have asked for in prayer has not happened, we step outside the will of God. You see, it is not our wisdom and worldly rationality that should make excuses. If we truly know who we are in Christ, we will also know that all we need to do is activate our faith, believe and it will without doubt be done. Hard though it certainly is in our natural thinking, we have to spiritually seek with all our heart why, just in case we are doing something to block a response, and in this seeking remain assured and convicted by God's ability and promises.

The Psalmist knew how to walk with God and left us with this sound advice:

'Trust in the Lord, and do good; so you will dwell in the land, and enjoy security. Take delight in the Lord, and he will give you the desires of your heart. Commit your way to the Lord; trust him, and he will act.' (Psalm 37: 3 – 5)

Delight, commitment and trust in God will cause Him to act!

'Therefore, since we are surrounded by so great a cloud of witnesses, let us also lay aside every weight, and sin which clings so closely, and let us run with perseverance the race that is set before us, looking to Jesus the pioneer and perfecter of our faith, who for the joy that was set before him endured the cross, despising the shame, and is seated at the right hand of the throne of God.' (Hebrews 12: 1, 2)

Food for Thought:

When we gave our life to Jesus we offered it to a Lord and Saviour who said, *'I came that they may have life, and have it abundantly'* (John 10: 10). This means we should live lives of supernatural abundance.

Chapter Seven

Ready for the Trumpet Call

'Watch therefore, for you do not know on what day your Lord is coming. But know this, that if the householder had known in what part of the night the thief was coming, he would have watched and would not have let his house be broken into. Therefore you also must be ready; for the Son of man is coming at an hour you do not expect.' (Matthew 24: 42 – 44)

Introduction

On two separate occasions nearly a year apart whilst out walking and talking with the Lord, He directed me to go and sit in a graveyard situated on one of my prayer walking routes. On the first occasion I was lead to look at the gravestones and read them.

What quickly occurred to me was the amount of times the term, 'Rest in peace' or similar sentiments were actually used. Here in front of me were fond memories of loved ones of different ages, fathers, mothers, sons, daughters, friends and relatives. Some had lived happy lives, others had lived in sadness. Some were well off, others struggled. Some were well-known and others lived inconspicuously. All shared one thing, they had lived and now their lives had ended. Opportunity and choices had come to an end. Sin in their lives had taken its toll.

As I pondered these various thoughts this horrible and shocking question passed through my mind, 'how many are actually resting in peace?' How many are actually in the terrible and everlasting torment of hell? How many of these people have the Church failed and the gospel message not been taught as it should have been taught? At that moment, the shocking reality of sin's destruction and separation from God made a deep impact upon me.

All of this was finally put into context when on the second occasion, as I briefly mentioned in chapter one, I sat looking at the hundreds of gravestones and whilst reflecting on my first experience I began to wonder how many of these souls were actually in Heaven.

I asked the Lord to show me how many in the graveyard I was sitting in were actually in Heaven. He directed me to walk along the first cross-section path. As I reached the third row of headstones the Lord stopped me. I looked left and right of where I was standing thinking that this indicated the Lord's answer. But He stopped me and said no, look to your left. This was toward the corner of the graveyard closest to the perimeter walls.

I was so shocked by the small number indicated by the Lord when compared with the entire graveyard that I questioned what I had heard and seen. When the Lord confirmed what I was looking at, even to my own surprise I broke down in uncontrollable tears as I saw no more than 1% of the cemetery in Heaven!

The Lord explained that there were people who had heard the gospel but who had rejected it. There were some that had not been taught the gospel message as it should have been diligently taught and there were many churchgoers and believers that thought they were okay but who had not fully committed themselves. The words of Jesus, *'be ready; for the Son of man is coming at an hour you do not expect'* (Matthew 24: 44) suddenly rang out loud and clear.

A Life Changing Message

Dear reader, I cannot over stress this point; being ready for the return of Jesus is one of, if not the most serious message that any Christian believer can receive. And yet amazingly I come across so many brothers and sisters in Christ who do not give it much credence and thought. In fact the second coming of our Lord for many is firmly tucked so far into the background of their thinking that it rarely sees the light of day. This, dear friend is not only tragic but spiritually foolish.

Now I am sure none of us really like being called foolish but this is exactly what Jesus Himself was saying about those that act like the foolish maidens found in Matthew 25: 1 – 13. It is not as if any of us have an excuse of ignorance or lack of knowledge that can claim we do not know that Jesus will return. We do know!

The problem is this; when thoughts of the return of Jesus coming back are hidden in the depths of our thinking we lose all sense of urgency. We easily fall prey to complacency, but, if we are eagerly looking with expectancy we stay alert, active and ready. The wise are those who are keeping themselves alert and ready. Are you among the foolish or the wise?

We must all firmly grasp that these words were actually spoken by Jesus and they are specifically meant for you and me, *what I say to you I say to all: Watch*' (Mark 13: 37). These words are among the most important any true Christian believer can hear and importantly, they are words we must positively respond to.

To highlight the point that I have made about actively watching for Jesus to return, what a tragedy it is when Christian believers who are asked what they would do if they knew Jesus was coming back at a certain time and date, say they would do everything they can to prepare. But then, they immediately forget the question and do nothing!

Can you begin to imagine what it would be like to find yourself left behind as you watch others being taken in front of your eyes when Jesus returns? I cannot emphasize the point too strongly. This message is no game. It is very serious and it will sadly cost the complacent, like the five foolish maidens, their spiritual lives.

The fact is, Jesus is coming for a bride eagerly watching and waiting; a bride without spot or blemish, a bride ready to literally be swept off their feet by the angels and caught up to Heaven at the trumpet blast. Are you eagerly ready? Are you watching?

We can learn much from Elisha. He would not let Elijah out of his sight. Everywhere Elijah went, Elisha followed. Elisha would not rest. He would not listen to distractions or allow himself to take his focus off Elijah. He just kept watch and eventually he saw Elijah taken to heaven. Only then did he receive Elijah's mantle (2 Kings 2: 1 - 14).

Elisha was totally focussed and determined. He was willing to pay the price of putting his own interests to one side so that he would receive God's blessing. Fittingly, Elijah's name means *Yahweh is my God* and Elisha's name means, *God is salvation!* Do not be fooled - far more is expected of you than a prayer to say you accept Jesus and then going once or twice a week to Church. Salvation costs you and me everything. There is no cheap or half-price ticket into Heaven.

With all of this in mind there is one thing we can continually be certain about; if Jesus said watch and be ready there is a very good reason He said it. If there is a reason for Jesus saying something then it is absolutely certain that we ought to know the reason, after all the information is clearly provided, and the signs are visibly obvious. It is our personal responsibility to watch and make ourselves ready.

Paul neatly summarized all of this in these words, *'be watchful, stand firm in your faith, be courageous, be strong. Let all that you do be done in love.'* (1 Corinthians 16: 13, 14). With these thoughts in mind it seems logical that we should first understand what the biblical word for watch actually means.

The Greek word for watch is **gregoreo** and means being vigilant, alert and awake, on guard, focused and watchful.

Far from being offensive, a heart of compassion leads me to say that it is a tragic and potentially costly dereliction of pastoral responsibility that most of our churches have, and sadly still are, failing to fully prepare their flock, members or congregations for the second coming of our Lord and Saviour Jesus Christ. It is also a solemn fact that many Christians have become blasé about the second coming of our Lord. Many pastors and ministers of God do not consider this an important message whilst others do not really understand it or its significance. Jesus however was very clear in his message and he said, *'Watch therefore, for you do not know on what day your Lord is coming. But know this, that if the householder had known in what part of the night the thief was coming, he would have watched and would not have let his house be broken into. Therefore you also must be ready; for the Son of man is coming at an hour you do not expect'* (Matthew 24: 42 – 44). When we die or Jesus returns it will be too late to argue about who is right and who is wrong. It will be too late if we are not ready.

Being ready means we are alert, we are suitably clothed, we have what we need, and we are completely prepared and watching for the moment to arrive. In all honesty, I do not know what the specifics are of God's intentions for the next couple of years. I do know that we must stand fully prepared and ready. I do know that God provides signs for us to watch and heed.

Part of our spiritual preparation starts with repentance and clearing the debris of sin from our lives which is why Paul said, *'Examine yourselves, to see whether you are holding to your faith. Test yourselves. Do you not realize that Jesus Christ is in you? – unless indeed you fail to meet the test!'* (2 Corinthians 13: 5, 6) If we do not look at ourselves and put ourselves to the test we will not know what our true spiritual condition is like. Why is this so important?

Testing Ourselves

What you are about to read is a message that has been totally ignored by the modern-day church and it has and is costing deceived believers their spiritual inheritance. Many Christians today make great assumptions about their heavenly inheritance based on the man-inspired teaching of flawed gospel messages and not on the truth of God's word. The love, prosperity and humanistic gospel messages are causing great harm.

Gospel messages that leave out details such as: repentance, the reality and devastation of sin, the truth of hell, the need to die to all self-will and that there are dark and hard times in our Christian walk are not telling the truth. Gospel messages that say: the more money and possessions you have are marks of your walk with God, or churches that tolerate or allow cursing, idol worship, anti-Semitism of any kind, humanistic influences and easy, laid-back lifestyles are deceptions.

Time and again Paul urges us to test or examine whether we are truly of the faith and sticking by it. And when writing to the church in Philippi Paul said, *'it has been granted to you that for the sake of Christ you should not only believe in him but also suffer for his sake, engaged in the same conflict which you saw and now hear to be mine'* (Philippians 1: 29, 30). Believing in Jesus will bring suffering!

The writer to the Hebrews explains that God chastens and disciplines His children in order to teach, train and mature them. It is of course painful for a while but, *'it yields the peaceful fruits of righteousness'* (Hebrews 12: 11) and so we are reminded:

> *'My son, do not regard lightly the discipline of the Lord, not lose courage when you are punished by him. For the Lord disciplines him whom he loves, and chastises every son whom he receives.'* (Hebrews 12: 5, 6)

Did you notice these words, *'the Lord disciplines him whom he loves, and chastises every son whom he receives'*? All those whom God loves are also disciplined. All those who are openly received by Him are chastised – yes, every one of them!

If we have not been chastised and spiritual trials and persecutions have not befallen us, such that we have to bear the cross of Jesus in some way, the writer of Hebrews makes this uncompromising statement: *'If you are left without discipline, in which all have participated, then you are illegitimate children and not sons'* (Hebrews 12: 8).

Put simply, the vital importance of regularly testing or examining ourselves is clearly explained by Paul in these words: *'to see whether or not you are holding to your faith'* (2 Corinthians 13: 5). What we need to understand is just as we look after our physical and mental health so we must also look after our spiritual health. There are many evil and man-inspired devices and influences that can knock us off course and away from the truth of God's word. Some are so subtle that it can take a long time to realize their dark secrets if we are not careful and diligent in our reading and study of Scripture. This is why the Bible is full of Scriptures that are checkpoints or spot checks designed to make us regularly assess our spiritual condition. The following are just a brief assortment for illustration purposes:

- Hebrews 2: 1 – *'Therefore we must pay the closer attention to what we have heard, lest we drift away from it.'*

- Luke 6: 46 – *'Why do you call me, 'Lord, Lord,' and not do what I tell you?'*

- Matthew 3: 8 – *'Bear fruit that befits repentance.'*

- John 13: 35 – *'By this all men will know that you are my disciples, if you have love for one another.'*

- Colossians 1: 10 – *'lead a life worthy of the Lord, fully pleasing to him, bearing fruit in every good work and increasing in the knowledge of God.'*

- John 15: 7 – *'If you abide in me, and my words abide in you, ask whatever you will, and it shall be done for you.'*

When we read these or similar Scriptures they should cause us to both immediately check where we stand and crucially, if necessary do something to make sure they are fulfilled in our lives.

These are also important because Jesus is coming for those, *'without spot or wrinkle or any such thing, that she [the church, each Christian believer] might be holy and without blemish'* (Ephesians 5: 27). The question should therefore surely be, 'what must I do?' And having answered this we must of course do what is necessary. The shocking reality is that few will look to themselves and perhaps even fewer will act to do whatever is actually needed; but why?

Unfortunately the cares of the world and the passage of time have made many believers complacent and so only a few are truly living in eager expectancy of the imminent return of Jesus. This situation, if it is one that any of us hold, is spiritually dangerous for at least two reasons:

- A lack of urgency leads to complacency and carelessness. In short, it leaves us off guard and open to attack and deception.

- As we can see from the parable of the ten maidens the state of unreadiness is foolish to the extreme. Trying to put our spiritual life right at the point when Jesus returns, is too late which is why Jesus left us with the warning to watch and remain ready.

The unarguable fact of biblical prophecy is that Jesus is going to come for his Bride, the Church. There will be a wonderful marriage supper for the Lamb and so we read *'Let us rejoice and exult and give him the glory, for the marriage of the Lamb has come, and his Bride has made herself ready; it was granted her to be clothed with fine linen, bright and pure – for the fine linen is the righteous deeds of the saints'* (Revelation 19: 7, 8). Did you notice that key message being proclaimed again *'**his Bride has made herself ready?**"* When we think about attending a wedding we can draw a number of parallels with the message of making ourselves ready for Jesus.

In our world, we first receive an invitation to the wedding. At this point we make a personal decision to either attend or decline the invite and we make this decision known to the invitees.

If we have accepted the invitation, then before the day of

the marriage, we will spend time thinking about how we will appropriately present ourselves and what type of gift we will give. We will go in search of that gift and of course a personal cost is always involved. The closer we are and the greater we honour the couple getting married the more we invest in them.

There are clear equivalents between an earthly wedding celebration and the spiritual celebration. We receive an invitation to either accept Jesus or to reject his offer. Those that have accepted the invitation, undertake spiritual preparation as they consider what they can give through faith and spiritual service. The more we love and esteem the Lord, the more we give of ourselves in realization that taking up the cross of Jesus brings with it a price, the price of worldly denial and giving all of self to Jesus (Luke 9: 23).

As we continue to think about the earthly and heavenly parallels of the wedding invitation, there is an important period of preparation and readiness for the big occasion and this takes time. It is not something we can rush. We need to make sure we have everything needed and we are 'spotlessly clean' and perfectly presentable.

If on the day of the wedding we oversleep, or have left everything to the last moment the chances are the door of the church will have closed and the service will already be underway before we get there!

Just as we need to wake up, take time to get ready and look the best we can for an earthly marriage, how much more time and effort will our spiritual marriage need? This is why we should live lives of constant readiness, vigilance, alertness and expectancy; expectant of the total fulfilment of God's promise that Jesus will return and that return will be soon.

Are You Ready?

I can make no apology for saying once again that this is probably the most important question facing every Christian believer today. It is not a question that any of us can briefly contemplate, give a few stock answers to and then immediately do nothing about. It is literally a spiritual 'life or death' question. It is a question that by its nature demands an answer because if we have not put everything in place to make sure we are ready, make no mistake, we will be left behind when the trumpet suddenly sounds!

Surely, the simple fact that we are talking about being ready suggests that something has to happen to bring us to a state of readiness? Surely, it is logical that if we are not ready it means we are going to miss out? So the question must surely be, what do we need to do to guarantee we are ready?

- Repent, *'and turn again, that your sins may be blotted out'* (Acts 3: 19). David was so aware of his need to confess, repent and ask forgiveness that from his heart he prayed Psalm 51. It is here where we see the depth of David's godly sorrow and regret over his sin. It is here where David humbly comes to God and confesses all his wickedness, repents and asks for forgiveness and restoration as he reaches out and says, *'Have mercy upon me, O God, According to Your loving kindness; According to the multitude of Your tender mercies, Blot out my transgressions. Wash me thoroughly from my iniquity, And cleanse me from my sin. For I acknowledge my transgressions, And my sin is ever before me. Against You, You only, have I sinned, And done this evil in Your sight – That you may be found just when You speak, And blameless when You judge'* (Psalm 51: 1 – 4 NKJV). It is this depth of shame and brokenness over sin, humility and repentance that we must reach. Anyone who has not truly repented is not ready because Jesus will return for those that are without spot, wrinkle or blemish (Ephesians 5: 27).

- Make Jesus Lord of your life, *'If then you have been raised with Christ, seek the things that are above, where Christ is, seated at the right hand of God. Set your minds on things that are above, not on things that are on earth. For you have died, and your life is hid with Christ in God'* (Colossians 3: 1 - 3). There is a plain and immoveable Scripture truth that we must all fully understand. Nobody can truly be ready for Jesus until, as Paul put it, *'you have died, and your life is hid with Christ in God'* (Colossians 3: 3). Those that are ready for Jesus have given up on worldly pleasures and gains. Jesus becomes our life as we realize that there is only one thing that has lasting value, eternal life.

- Die to self, *'I have been crucified with Christ; it is no longer I who live, but Christ who lives in me; and the life I now live in the flesh I live by faith in the Son of God, who loved me and gave himself for me'* (Galatians 2: 20). We must die to self and be 'raised with Christ.' Those that are ready for Jesus have willingly crucified themselves and now focus their eyes intently on Heaven.

Paul also made this incredible statement of total commitment, *'the world has been crucified to me, and I to the world'* (Galatians 6: 14). Paul was so committed and dedicated to Jesus that worldly things, as far as he was concerned had been firmly nailed to the cross. He was now living in the Spiritual realm; holiness and Heaven. He separated himself from the world in a way that we too should earnestly seek.

- Fulfil the command, *'love one another; even as I have loved you'* (John 13: 34), this means putting away evil thoughts and words spoken against others, including other ministries, denominations and the Jewish people.

John explains that, *'love is of God, and he who loves is born of God and knows God. He who does not love does not know God; for God is love'* (1 John 4: 7, 8). Anyone who does not love in thought, word and action does not know God and they are not ready.

Peter reminds us that *'The end of all things is at hand'* (1 Peter 4: 7). That statement is relevant to each one of us and part of our readiness for Jesus is wrapped-up in what Peter said following this statement:

'...hold unfailing your love for one another, since love covers

a multitude of sins. Practice hospitality ungrudgingly to one another. As each has received a gift, employ it for one another, as good stewards of God's varied grace.' (1 Peter 4: 8 – 10)

What Peter was actually saying is, show deep love for one another because this covers a multitude of sins. The Greek word for cover used in this text is **kalypto**, which means to hide, mask or veil. Sin may exist but by our actions toward one another we love anyway and help to deal with these as good stewards.

• Forgive, *'put them all away: anger, wrath, malice, slander, and foul talk from your mouth'* (Colossians 3: 8) and *'forbearing one another and, if one has a complaint against another, forgiving each other; as the Lord has forgiven you, so you must also forgive'* (Colossians 3: 13). Scripture cannot be clearer, we must resolve all disputes, grudges, bitterness and hurts. If we fail to do this we are not ready for the return of Jesus. And Jesus also said, *'if you do not forgive men their trespasses, neither will your Father forgive your trespasses'* (Matthew 6: 15).

• Be holy, *'strive for peace with all men, and for the holiness without which no one will see the Lord'* (Hebrews 12: 14). It is because God is holy that we, His children must also be holy.

The truth of who we are because of Jesus our Lord and Saviour is clearly articulated by Peter in these words:

'But you are a chosen race, a royal priesthood, a holy nation, God's own people, that you may declare the wonderful deeds of him who called you out of darkness into his marvellous light. Once you were no people but now you are God's people; once you had not received mercy but now you have received mercy.' (1 Peter 2: 9, 10)

If we are not thirsting for holiness we do not truly know who we are as a royal priesthood. Did you notice that we are not just called the priesthood; we are a royal priesthood with specific rights to come into the very heart and presence of God. As dedicated servants we are completely set apart from worldliness and sin to form a spiritual relationship with God through the willing presentation of our bodies as holy, living sacrifices, which Paul described as our spiritual worship in Romans 12: 1. If we have not presented our bodies as living sacrifices we are not ready.

- Walk in faith, *'without faith it is impossible to please him'* (Hebrews 11: 6). Walking by faith is about believing what God says is absolutely true.

Jesus outlined the basis of faith in these words:

'Have faith in God. Truly, I say to you, whoever says to this mountain, 'Be taken up and cast into the sea,' and does not doubt in his heart, but believes that what he says will come to pass, it will be done for him.' (Mark 11: 22, 23)

The incredible truth about our Heavenly heritage if we are to live as God intends, is that these words of Jesus recorded in Mark's gospel are biblical examples of God's word and will for each of us. Everything Jesus said and did during the course of His life is an example of what you and I can and should say and do in our daily lives.

If we have not done these things and don't live in them day by day, we are not ready. Why? If these things have not been dealt with it is a sign that we have not cooperated fully with God. We must decide if we are going to give our life in its entirety to God or not. We must decide if we are willing (or not) to pay whatever the cost to walk as God wants of us.

David knew how much he had offended God because of his selfish sin. He understood the level of commitment that is necessary and so, from his heart of repentance he said, *'Purge me with hyssop, and I shall be clean; Wash me, and I shall be whiter than snow. Make me to hear joy and gladness, That the bones which You have broken may rejoice. Hide your face from my sins, And blot out all my iniquities. Create in me a clean heart, O God, And renew a steadfast spirit within me'* (Psalm 51: 7 – 11).

It is not about pointing a finger at others or criticising them, it is about putting our own lives in order. We are all sinners and so we all need to earnestly pray this prayer over our lives so that we remain close to God's heart.

Staying Ready

Being drawn away from God is something that we are often warned about during the last days, *'men will be lovers of self, lovers of money, proud, arrogant, abusive, disobedient to their parents, ungrateful, unholy, inhuman, implacable, slanderers, profligates, fierce, haters of good, treacherous, reckless, swollen with conceit, lovers of pleasure rather than lovers of God, holding the form of religion but denying the power of it'* (2 Timothy 3: 2 – 5). We cannot be ready for Jesus if we do not have our relationship with God, Jesus and the Holy Spirit in good order. In his first letter John says, *'abide in him, so that when he appears we may have confidence and not shrink from him in shame at his coming'* (1 John 2: 28). The Greek word for abide is **meno** meaning to endure with, stay with or abide with; today we might say to fellowship with.

The call is for us to stay firmly focused on God and not be distracted by satan's wiles and enticements. The story of Lot's wife is a frightening and stern warning about not keeping our eyes on God. Let's take a chilling look at this unheeded warning.

Due to their grave sin, God's wrath came upon the Dead Sea valley of Siddim and the cities of Sodom and Gomorrah. But because of Lot's faithfulness, the Lord was merciful to Lot and his family and allowed them to escape the judgment, warning them to flee and not to look back. We then read these words, *'Then the Lord rained on Sodom and Gomorrah brimstone and fire from (the Lord) out of heaven; and he overthrew those cities, and all the valley, and all the inhabitants of the cities, and what grew on the ground. But Lot's wife behind him looked back, and she became a pillar of salt'*

(Genesis 19: 24 – 26). Lot's wife was tantalizingly close to being saved and preserved but at the last moment she disobeyed, took her eyes off God and looked back.

When the disciples asked Jesus when the end of all things will take place and what the signs will be he responded by saying, *'take heed that no one leads you astray'* (Matthew 24: 4) and *'he who endures to the end will be saved'* (Matthew 24: 13). The primary concern of Jesus was that they guard against being led astray and that they keep the faith until the end. In other words, we are not safe until we endure to the end.

Jesus warned us to take heed of his words, to look for the signs, watch and be faithful. There are a number of New Testament Scriptures which tell us about watching. Let's prayerfully consider each of these:

- Matthew 26: 41 – *'Watch and pray that you may not enter into temptation; the spirit indeed is willing, but the flesh is weak.'*

- Luke 21: 34 - 36 – *'Take heed to yourselves lest your hearts be weighed down with dissipation [carousing or indulging in physical pleasures] and drunkenness and cares of this life, and that day come upon you suddenly like a snare; for it will come upon all who dwell upon the face of the whole earth. But watch at all times, praying that you may have strength to escape all these things that will take place, and to stand before the Son of man.'*

- 1 Corinthians 16: 13 – *'Be watchful, stand firm in your faith, be courageous, be strong.'*

- Ephesians 6: 18 – *'Pray at all times in the Spirit, with all prayer and supplication. To that end keep alert with all perseverance, making supplications for all the saints.'*

- Colossians 4: 2 – *'Continue steadfastly in prayer, being watchful in it with thanksgiving.'*

- 1 Peter 5: 8 – *'Be sober, be watchful. Your adversary the*

*devil prowls around like a roaring lion, seeking someone to
devour.'*

As Hezekiah discovered there are times when God will leave
us to test what we will do and what is in our heart (2 Chronicles 32: 31).
We are living in days where God is watching our obedience to the
words of Jesus. To watch, pray and stand firm. There will be times
when those around us will isolate us as we seek to go deeper with
God. We will have to wrestle like Jacob did if we want the blessings
of God – our determination will need to prove that we will not let
go until God grants His blessing and His supernatural power.

Of course we must also not forget the second commandment
to love others as ourselves. Loving God is but part of the equation.
Actually we cannot love God without also loving others. John
makes this point, *'we know that we have passed out of death into life,
because we love the brethren. He who does not love abides in death.
Anyone who hates his brother is a murderer, and you know that no
murderer has eternal life abiding in him'* (1 John 3: 14, 15). John goes on
to say, *'let us not love in word or speech but in deed and in truth'* (1
John 3: 18). What we do, what we say and what we think of others is
the measure of our love for them. If any of this falls short of God's
love we are failing to obey the commandment and we are not ready
for Jesus.

I could not hope to bring this chapter to a close in any better
way than with the words of the second letter of Peter who wrote, *'I
have aroused your sincere mind by way of reminder; that you should
remember the predictions of the holy prophets and the commandment
of the Lord and Saviour through your apostles'* (2 Peter 3: 1, 2). Peter
goes on to say that there will be scoffers who will say, *'where is
the promise of his coming?'* (v4). Let us not get tangled up in their
propaganda and 'tittle-tattle.' We must look expectantly for Jesus
to return and make sure we live repentant lives. Peter urges that we
consider what sort of person we should really be, *'in lives of holiness
and godliness, waiting for and hastening the coming of the day of
God'* (v11, 12).

Being ready means we strive for holiness, peace and love.
We must take care not to get caught up in the teachings of those

who twist the Scriptures to fit their own ends but rather preach the undiluted gospel message in faith and with demonstrable power.

Prophecy

In 2011, I included this prophecy in a publication The Language of Love, Forgiveness, Faith, Prayer and Healing (Onwards and Upwards)

There is a fresh wave of God's power coming and we are now at the brink of it; this revival will outstretch any other revival. It will be worldwide and based upon the word of God, dedication to prayer, the power of the Holy Spirit and love reaching deep into local communities.

God will seek out those who will boldly teach the undiluted word with compassion and love. A fresh breed of pastor will protect the flock, seek the lost and the wandering and the church will become a house of prayer - both as a congregation and in private homes.

Leaders will be challenged to let go of 'their' work and allow God to move by His Spirit. God's people will be released to exercise their God-given gifts and move through local communities, meeting needs in love and the power of the Holy Spirit. The blessings of God will flow and healings will release captives.

Soon after this Jesus will come for His Bride.

'And now I commend you to God and to the word of his grace, which is able to build you up and give you the inheritance among all those who are sanctified.' (Acts 20: 32)

Food for Thought:

Will you say 'I wish I had'? Or will it be, 'I'm glad I did'?

Conclusion

'He has shown you, O man, what is good; and what does the LORD require of you but to do justice, and to love kindness, and to walk humbly with your God?' (Micah 6: 8)

This is a message specifically for those who are true followers of Christ and covenant children of God. The message was delivered by Isaiah's contemporary, Micah whose name means 'like God (Yhwh).' He was a man of strong conviction, courage and personality who said of himself, *'I am filled with power, with the Spirit of the LORD, and with justice and might'* (Micah 3: 8).

Being like God, Micah was a man of love. He also possessed spiritual attributes that are sorely needed in abundance for these last of the last days. God is calling people like you and me to stand in the vanguard of what He intends to do before Jesus returns. The question is, are you willing to selflessly answer the call?

In many ways the time in which Micah wrote these words mirrors that in which we are living today. Society was full of corruption, economic crimes, swindling and mistrust as those in positions of power oppressed the weak.

Priests taught for personal gain and prophets led many people astray with their false and diluted teaching. As a result of this most believers were living under the shadow of a 'dead', or impotent faith. Holiness was a scarce commodity of those who believed in God.

The earnestness, total commitment and trust in God were in word but missing in action and in heart belief. Where people did realize the true degradation of sins in their lives, they were totally prepared to give their bodies as sacrifice but in this they misunderstood God's heart and purpose.

Amazingly and with such love and mercy even amidst the floundering and faltering faith environment God offered a better and greater way to attain meaningful restoration and renewal with Him:

- To do justice. The Hebrew word for justice is **mishpat** and literally means to act like a judge in the sense of acting justly and doing what is right. It is about believers living lives that do what is right in all their dealings before God and humankind.

- To love kindness. **Checed** is the Hebrew word used in this context for kindness. It means to act with mercy, compassion and good deeds.

- To walk humbly. Here the Hebrew word used by Micah is **tsana**, which means living lives of humility, modesty and lowliness or submission before God. It is about putting all self-interest aside and living as God leads.

The choices we make and the life we live now not only shape the person we are here on earth but they have eternal consequences. Short-term pain is worth long-term gain.

Underpinning everything written in this book is the urgent need for every true Christian believer to deal with sin in their lives. None of us will make headway spiritually whilst the shackles of sin and worldly living hold us down.

Speaking about our origins Jesus said:

'You are of your father the devil, and your will is to do your father's desires. He was a murderer from the beginning, and has nothing to do with the truth, because there is no truth in him. When he lies, he speaks according to his own nature, for he is a liar and the father of lies.' (John 8: 44)

Satan can do nothing but tell lies because that is his nature. There is nothing good that comes from him. His sweet-smelling lures are nothing more than elaborate traps. He is like the Venus flytrap, the carnivorous consumer of the unsuspecting insects seeking to devour all that come into contact. Make no mistake; at any opportunity satan will take your spiritual life unless you are hid in Christ.

If we love righteousness and hate sin, God will 'fall over Himself' to anoint us with gladness. He will open His Heavenly treasures to us. The Psalmist put what I am trying to say this way:

'Come and hear, all you who fear God, and I will tell you what he has done for me. I cried aloud to him, and he was extolled with my tongue. If I had cherished iniquity in my heart, the Lord would not have listened. But truly God has listened; he has given heed to the voice of my prayer.' (Psalm 66: 16 – 19)

Sin is an issue in our lives that we must deal with whilst we still have opportunity. Now is the time for repentance. Now is the time to put our spiritual house in order. Jesus is coming soon and he is coming for those that it says in Hebrews 9:28 are eagerly looking for him; those that Paul described in Ephesians 5:27 as without spot, wrinkle or blemish.

'Let us know, let us press on to know the LORD; his going forth is sure as the dawn; he will come to us as the showers, as the spring rains that water the earth.' (Hosea 6: 3)

Prayer

Bring abundant blessing and peace Lord to all those who humbly read these words inspired from Your heart and may Your name always be glorified and Your purposes fulfilled.

I believe You are true to your word Lord and You will touch all those who enter these pages, seek You with all their heart and apply these messages to their lives. Bring healing to their life, open the eyes of the blind and set every captive free.

And Finally…

This has been a message specifically for those who are seeking a closer walk with the Lord. The book has concluded with the repeated message of repentance and dealing with sin in our lives so that we walk as children of light.

John wrote: *'if we walk in the light, as he is in the light, we have fellowship with one another, and the blood of Jesus his Son cleanses us from all sin.'* (1 John 1: 7)

It has been my honour and privilege to serve the Lord and connect in fellowship with you through these pages.

Where ever you are in the world, I pray the Lord's hand of favour upon you and look forward to meeting you, if not here on earth, with our blessed Lord in the Kingdom of Heaven.

Shalom

Leon Gosiewski

About Dunamis Fire Ministries

Dunamis Fire Ministries are a prayer and faith-based, non-profit, international healing and teaching ministry.

God's mandate on this ministry is to prepare souls for the return of Jesus by opening 'the eyes that are blind, to bring out the prisoners from the dungeon, from the prison those who sit in darkness' (Isaiah 42: 7) and set captives free.

The calling of this ministry is to heal the Church and part of this healing involves stirring the Church to awaken, to get ready and to prepare for the second coming of the Lord. Leon's premise is faith in the Lord and 'believe, just believe.'

To contact the author please write to:

Leon Gosiewski
Dunamis Fire Ministries
Bethel Media House
Tobermore
Magherafelt
Northern Ireland
BT45 5SG (UK)

Visit www.dunamisfire.com

E. info@dunamisfire.com

Study Notes

These study notes have been included to make available to readers a study guide based on the important messages contained in this book. The study notes are suitable for individuals or those who are part of a discussion or Bible study group.

This study guide has been presented in the following format:

Pre-preparation for the study - Read the chapter and take notes

Preparing to hear from God – It is important to take time to open our spiritual ears, hearts and minds to what God wants to say. Time in prayer gives us an opportunity to both speak with God and listen to Him.

Reading the Word of God – When reading Bible passages, read them slowly and out loud. Take time to think about the words and what they mean.

The study – A brief summary of each chapter is provided. This is followed by a few questions to think about or discuss.

Chapter one

'Now to him who by the power at work in us is able to do far more abundantly than all that we ask or think, to him be glory in the church and in Christ Jesus to all generations, for ever and ever. Amen.' (Ephesians 3: 20, 21)

In this opening chapter every true Christian believer is plainly brought face-to-face with a message that has been concealed from our focus for far too long. The message is that in literally everything we do and say as members of Christ's Body, we must glorify God. And so it was that Paul explained this vital obligation by saying: *'whatever you do, in word or deed, do everything in the name of the Lord Jesus, giving thanks to God the Father through him'* (Colossians 3:17).

The world should constantly be attracted by the warm light and life of Jesus that glows from us, and not be appalled by the cold darkness and lifelessness of our worldliness. The truth revealed in this chapter will show a powerful key that will open the door to who we really are.

Questions:

- What does 'to glorify God' mean?
- Why has the message to glorify God in our lives been lost?
- What has been mis-sold about being a true Christian?
- What must I do to shine the light of the Lord through my life?
- What are the keys that open the door to who I really am?

NOTES:

Chapter two

'Do not be conformed to this world but be transformed by the renewal of your mind, that you may prove what is the will of God, what is good and acceptable and perfect.' (Romans 12: 2)

What and who we were spiritually before Jesus came into our lives, must die so that we become what Paul described as, *'a new creation'* (2 Corinthians 5:17). The process starts when we truly give our lives to Christ. But there is another side to our new life in Christ that must be broken and submitted. It is for this reason that chapter two concentrates on the vital importance of this dynamic step.

Questions:

- Why must I die to self-interests, attitudes and worldly living?
- What does it mean to 'truly' give our lives to Christ?
- What is the outcome of remaining conformed to the world?
- What does being transformed by the renewing of our mind mean?
- Study Colossians chapter three

NOTES:

Chapter three

'If my people who are called by my name humble themselves, and pray and seek my face, and turn from their wicked ways, then I will hear from heaven, and will forgive their sin and heal their land.' (2 Chronicles 7: 14)

Of course, because of our sinful upbringing, there are issues that will come into sharper focus as the light of God's word and His holy presence shine upon us. Not least of these, is the need for each one of us to face the humbling necessity to unshackle from our past, because God is taking us where worldly things cannot go! When we learn this fact, doors that were once closed will now open!

Questions:

- What does it really mean to humble ourselves?
- What does repentance really mean?
- What are the hallmarks of repentance?
- Why is forgiveness important?

NOTES:

Chapter four

'See to it that no one fail to obtain the grace of God; that no 'root of bitterness' spring up and cause trouble, and by it the many become defiled.' (Hebrews 12: 15)

This remarkable chapter highlights a key ingredient that God has made freely available to us. The fact that this gift is made available to us at all is so astonishing and incomprehensible for the believer that in 1773 the poet, hymn writer and priest John Newton (1725 – 1807) wrote one of our most famous hymns that to this day is still widely sung, "Amazing Grace". Learning how to wrap ourselves in this gift makes the Christian walk powerfully effective!

Questions:

- What are the lessons that we can learn from a shepherd?
- The role of a shepherd is to preserve life. How does this apply to us?
- What is God's grace?
- How do we obtain the great grace of God?

NOTES:

Chapter five

'I therefore, a prisoner for the Lord, beg you to lead a life worthy of the calling to which you have been called.' (Ephesians 4: 1)

Just as there is no division between God, Jesus and the Holy Spirit so no divisions and disagreements should exist among us. But why is it that on one hand we become one family with brothers and sisters and yet on the opposite hand we have criticism and fragmentation within the church? Learning to step into the fire of His glory will extinguish the counterfeit flames of division and give hope to a dying world.

Questions:

- What did Paul mean when he said, 'lead a life worthy of the calling'?
- Why are words powerful in their effect?
- Paul outlined the requirements of leading a life worthy of our calling in Ephesians 4: 1 – 3. What are they and why are they important?

NOTES:

Chapter six

'I say to you, rise, take up your pallet and go home.' And he rose, and immediately took up the pallet and went out before them all; so that they were all amazed and glorified God, saying, 'We never saw anything like this!' (Mark 2: 11, 12)

Was it simply a throw-away statement when Jesus said, "Truly, truly, I say to you, he who believes in me will also do the works that I do; and greater works than these will he do, because I go to the Father" (John 14: 12). After all Jesus did go to His Father so why is the church not doing 'greater works?' Being in Christ demands evidence and we explored why in this chapter.

Questions:

- What does it mean to walk in God's supernatural power?
- How can we walk in God's supernatural power?
- What does it mean to hunger and thirst after God?

NOTES:

Chapter seven

'Watch therefore, for you do not know on what day your Lord is coming. But know this, that if the householder had known in what part of the night the thief was coming, he would have watched and would not have let his house be broken into. Therefore you also must be ready; for the Son of man is coming at an hour you do not expect.' (Matthew 24: 42 – 44)

What will it be like when the clouds roll back, the trumpet sounds and the King of kings appears? More importantly how will we be viewed as the church? Will we be found without spot and wrinkle? Is it possible to cross from this life into Heaven without tasting death? What if the return of the Lord is in our lifetime? Will we be ready for the trumpet call? The last days crescendo waits!

Questions:

- Why must we constantly keep alert and watch for the return of Jesus?
- The summary above poses several questions. Work through each of these.

NOTES: